How to Heal Your Inner Child

CRAFTED BY SKRIUWER

For more information, contact : **kontakt@skriuwer.com** (www.skriuwer.com)

TABLE OF CONTENTS

CHAPTER 6: BREAKING HARMFUL PATTERNS

- *How early-life habits turn into adult roadblocks*
- *Identifying recurring cycles that harm well-being*
- *Replacing old patterns with healthier alternatives*
- *Forgiving yourself and moving forward*

CHAPTER 7: HEALTHY BOUNDARIES

- *Definition and purpose of personal boundaries*
- *Recognizing boundary gaps from childhood*
- *Steps to set and communicate limits*
- *Managing pushback and preserving self-respect*

CHAPTER 8: HANDLING SHAME AND GUILT

- *Distinguishing guilt (action-based) from shame (self-based)*
- *Tracing negative beliefs to childhood events*
- *Safe ways to process deep regrets or blame*
- *Releasing or reducing toxic shame for inner calm*

CHAPTER 9: RELATIONSHIPS AND SUPPORT SYSTEMS

- *Importance of genuine connection for emotional health*
- *Choosing safe and respectful people in your circle*
- *Overcoming fear of closeness rooted in past hurts*
- *Balancing self-reliance with supportive ties*

CHAPTER 10: OVERCOMING FEAR

- *How fear develops and when it becomes limiting*
- *Emotional and physical effects of too much fear*
- *Practical tools for easing and managing anxiety*
- *Why overcoming fear boosts inner child trust*

CHAPTER 11: SELF-WORTH

- *Defining self-worth beyond performance or praise*
- *Signs of low self-value and their childhood roots*
- *Daily habits to rebuild a sense of personal importance*
- *Connecting self-worth to a stronger inner identity*

CHAPTER 18: HELPFUL ROUTINES FOR HEALING

- *Daily and weekly habits that anchor emotional health*
- *Designing routines to fit personal needs and time*
- *Overcoming boredom or discouragement*
- *Making consistent habits that calm the inner child*

CHAPTER 19: PERSONAL GROWTH STRATEGIES

- *Key mindsets for steady improvement*
- *Breaking large goals into small actionable steps*
- *Trying new experiences to expand comfort zones*
- *Using reflection and emotional regulation for progress*

CHAPTER 20: LONG-TERM MAINTENANCE

- *Sustaining progress when life changes arise*
- *Avoiding relapse into old harmful patterns*
- *Keeping the inner child safe and reassured*
- *Maintaining routines, goals, and support networks for ongoing well-being*

CHAPTER 1: UNDERSTANDING THE CONCEPT OF THE INNER CHILD

Introduction

Every person has a side that feels younger than their age. Some people call this the "inner child." It is not a physical child living inside you. Instead, it is a set of emotions, ideas, and memories from childhood that stay active in your current life. Even if you are fully grown, this part can show up in how you respond to problems, stress, and even moments of joy.

Many people think of growing up as a process of leaving childhood behind. Yet our minds hold onto experiences—both good and bad—from our early years. If you had a very loving family, your inner child can feel safe and trusting. If your childhood had hardship, your inner child may feel scared, angry, or withdrawn. When we do not know about this part of ourselves, we may wonder why we have certain habits or strong emotional reactions that appear out of nowhere.

Why You Should Learn About Your Inner Child

Knowing about your inner child helps you see patterns in your life. For example, if you grew up in an environment where adults did not give you attention, you might still feel that no one hears you. When you face a conflict at work or in a relationship, you may react strongly if you feel ignored, as if you are trying to fix what happened in the past.

Learning about your inner child also helps you handle unresolved pain. This can include:

- Feeling like you are not important.
- Feeling anxious in social situations.
- Having sudden anger or sadness triggered by small things.
- Acting out of old fears even when they are no longer relevant.

When you become aware of the inner child, you can start to give it the care it did not receive before. That might mean telling yourself words of comfort when you feel unsafe. It may also mean saying no to things that harm you or setting new boundaries in your relationships.

Common Misunderstandings

1. "I had a normal childhood. Why do I need this?"
Even if your childhood was calm, no one grows up without at least a few misunderstandings, hurts, or regrets. When you ignore the child part of yourself, you may miss out on feeling good about who you are.

2. "Focusing on my childhood is just blaming the past."
It is not about blaming anyone. It is about noticing how certain events shaped your thinking and emotions. You do not have to hold grudges. Instead, you can see how your past connects to your present reactions.

3. "The past is gone. Why not move on?"
Yes, the past is gone. But your feelings about the past may remain. Learning to face them can free you to live with more peace in the present.

Important Clues That Your Inner Child Needs Attention

There are certain signs that your inner child might be in distress:

1. **Feeling Overly Reactive**: If a small setback makes you feel extremely upset, it may be the child part of you reacting.
2. **Constant Need for Approval**: Perhaps you feel uneasy if someone does not praise your work, and you look for external approval to feel okay.
3. **Guilt and Shame**: You may feel guilty over things that are not your fault, or you might feel worthless without logical reasons.
4. **Fear of Abandonment**: You might worry that the people close to you will leave, even when there is no evidence for this.
5. **Difficulty Being Alone**: Some people avoid being alone because they feel it brings up old fears.

If any of these describe your experience, it may help to look at your inner child more closely.

Key Differences Between the Adult Self and the Inner Child

As an adult, you have more control and perspective than you did as a child. You can pay bills, make rational decisions, and plan for the future. The child part of you does not think in a rational way. It sees the world in terms of feelings, safety, or danger. Here is how they might differ:

1. **Adult Self**: Usually follows logic. Considers time, responsibilities, and consequences.
2. **Inner Child**: Driven by raw feelings. Focuses on being safe, loved, and seen.

When you feel mixed or confusing feelings, it might be these two sides battling each other. By understanding the needs of your inner child, you can use your adult self to bring calm and care to those deeper emotions.

Noticing Common Childhood Wounds

Childhood wounds are often formed when we are too young to handle strong feelings or events. Some examples include:

- **Loss of a caregiver**: This can lead to fear that people you love will vanish.
- **Being bullied**: This can lead to distrust of peers and a fear of judgment.
- **Physical or emotional abuse**: This can lead to low self-esteem and an inability to feel safe in relationships.
- **Having a caregiver who was emotionally distant**: This can lead to difficulty expressing feelings or trusting others.

These old wounds can shape your adult thoughts and behavior more than you realize.

How the Brain Stores Childhood Experiences

The brain organizes memories so we can make sense of the world. When you are little, your brain is still developing. You depend on adults for safety. If you face events that feel unsafe, your brain may create a protective response. Over time, these protective responses become habits. In adulthood, the same triggers might activate those habits, even though you are no longer a child.

Example: If you were scolded harshly every time you tried something new, you might have learned to stay quiet. Now, as an adult, you might hold back from sharing new ideas at work out of a hidden fear of being embarrassed.

How Awareness Begins the Healing Process

The first step in healing is to notice when your child side is reacting. Recognize that this child side is neither weak nor silly. It is part of who you are, and it is shaped by early life events. By being aware, you can start to give it the support it needs.

We will not use complicated methods here. You just need to notice yourself during emotional situations. Ask:

- "Am I reacting like the grownup me or like the child me?"
- "What old feeling is this moment stirring up?"
- "What did I need back then that I did not get?"

You might begin to see a pattern. This can be a turning point. Instead of judging yourself, you can offer kindness to that child part.

A Few Lesser-Known Ideas About the Inner Child (Potential "Golden" Insights)

1. **Sensory Triggers**: Sometimes, smells, sounds, or lights can set off old feelings. This is because the senses strongly link to memories. Not many people realize how simple cues can spark old emotional states.
2. **Body-Based Signals**: Tension in the shoulders, stomach aches, or sudden headaches can be a clue that your inner child is anxious. Recognizing physical signals is important.
3. **Protective Imagination**: Children often cope with pain by imagining safe places or scenarios. As an adult, you can use short visualization moments to calm yourself. This method taps into that same imaginative power you had as a child.
4. **Old Belief Systems**: Children sometimes blame themselves for events they cannot control. This can lead to beliefs like, "I caused the problem." Even though you are an adult, you might be carrying these beliefs without noticing.

Practical Steps to Connect with Your Inner Child

1. **Create a Photo Reminder**: If possible, find a photo of yourself as a child and keep it somewhere you can see it. When you feel upset, look at it and remember that part of you needs comfort.
2. **Name the Feeling**: When emotions rise, instead of pushing them away, name them: "I feel worried," "I feel sad," or "I feel lonely." Naming the feeling can calm the mind.

3. **Speak Gentle Words to Yourself**: You can say things like: "It's okay, you are safe now," or "You did not deserve that back then." It might feel odd at first, but it helps.
4. **Seek Knowledge, Not Blame**: As you look at your past, try to learn what happened and how it affects you now. Avoid blaming yourself. The child within you did not know better.

How These Steps Will Help in the Next Chapters

The chapters that follow will explore deeper layers of emotional pain and how to address them. You will see how to spot your triggers, change harmful patterns, and practice healthy ways to handle shame, guilt, and fear. You will also learn to build supportive networks around you.

Before moving on, remember that accepting your inner child is a valuable step toward overall emotional health. It allows you to grow as an adult while caring for the younger side that still exists within you.

CHAPTER 2: RECOGNIZING PAST HURTS

Introduction

Many people struggle with how to see their past in a clear way. It can be hard to look back on old memories, especially if they carry pain. But spotting the hurts that formed during childhood is an important step. It gives you the chance to handle the root causes of your worries, sadness, or anger, instead of just reacting on the surface.

In this chapter, we will focus on methods to identify past hurts. We will also talk about how your mind hides certain memories to protect you. By the end, you should have a clearer sense of what might be influencing your present feelings and behavior.

Why Do Past Hurts Hide?

Your mind is designed to protect you from strong emotional pain. It can do this by "forgetting" certain events, or by making you think those events were not a big deal. These defense mechanisms work well when you are young and unable to address the pain. However, in adulthood, those hidden memories can cause confusion.

Example: A child who gets scolded harshly might start to think, "I am not allowed to speak up." As an adult, you may avoid sharing important thoughts because deep down, you think your voice is not welcome. You might not even recall the original scolding that caused this view.

Signs of Hidden Past Hurts

1. **Unexplained Sadness or Anger**: If you feel a wave of sorrow or anger that seems to come from nowhere, it may come from old pain.
2. **Overreaction to Small Issues**: You might break down or get furious over something minor.
3. **Chronic Anxiety**: You feel tense most of the time, even when there is no direct threat.

4. **Trouble with Trust**: You may have a habit of doubting others' words or actions without evidence.

When you notice these signs, it is helpful to think about whether they link to old events.

Common Areas of Childhood Hurt

- **Emotional Neglect**: If your caregivers did not show warmth or did not notice your needs, you could grow up feeling invisible.
- **Harsh Criticism**: Children who are criticized too often can develop a sense of never being good enough.
- **Unfair Comparisons**: Being constantly compared to siblings or peers can lead to feeling inferior.
- **Instability in the Home**: If the household was chaotic, you might still struggle with feeling safe in adult life.
- **Bullying by Peers**: Early bullying can lead to long-term social anxiety or a fear of groups.

Methods to Identify Your Past Hurts

1. **Journaling**: Writing about your childhood can be a powerful tool. You can do it in bullet points or short paragraphs. Try to recall an event from childhood each day and note the emotions you felt then.
2. **Drawing**: If writing seems too direct, try drawing simple sketches of your childhood environment. Draw your house, your school, or the faces of people you remember. You do not have to be an artist. The act of drawing might spark memories you forgot.
3. **Body Scan**: Focus on different parts of your body, such as your neck, shoulders, arms, chest, stomach, and legs. Notice if any area feels tense when you think about certain memories. This can reveal hidden emotions.
4. **Mindful Questioning**: Ask yourself simple questions: "When was the earliest time I recall feeling unworthy?" "Who was around me then?" "What did they say or do?" Take notes if any memory surfaces.
5. **Safe Conversations**: Share childhood stories with a trusted friend, family member, or professional. Sometimes, speaking out loud helps bring clarity.

Handling the Emotions That Appear

As you uncover your past hurts, you might feel sadness, anger, or even shame. This is normal. You are looking at events that caused harm. Though uncomfortable, this step is necessary to break free from old patterns.

A few ideas to help you handle these emotions:

1. **Calming Techniques**: Take slow, deep breaths. Inhale for four counts, hold for two counts, and exhale for four counts. Do this a few times. This can reduce stress and help you focus.
2. **Grounding Tools**: Observe your surroundings. Name five things you see around you, four things you can hear, three things you can touch, two things you can smell, and one thing you can taste. This can bring you back to the present if the memories feel too intense.
3. **Positive Self-Talk**: Remind yourself you are no longer in that situation. You are older and have more power now.

Lesser-Known Insights on Identifying Past Hurts (Potential "Golden" Info)

1. **Memory Gaps**: Sometimes, you might discover you cannot recall large chunks of your childhood. The brain sometimes blocks out traumatic or painful memories. Realizing you have memory gaps can be a clue that something significant happened.
2. **Hidden Emotional Contracts**: Children may form promises or "contracts" in their minds like, "I will never let anyone hurt me again by speaking too loudly." These silent vows can show up in adult life as avoidance or aggression.
3. **Cultural Factors**: In some cultures, children are taught not to speak about family problems. This can lead to hidden hurts that are never acknowledged. It is important to recognize if cultural norms shaped your silence about childhood events.
4. **Erratic Physical Reactions**: Strange body reactions—like feeling sick to your stomach when thinking of certain people—may point to past hurts. The mind and body are connected, and the body often sends signals when memories are too painful for the mind to process directly.

How to Confirm If a Memory Is True or Not

Sometimes, people worry that they might be recalling events incorrectly. Memory can be imperfect, especially under stress. However, you do not have to confirm every detail. The main goal is to understand how you felt then and how it affects you now. If a certain recollection leaves you feeling very upset, then it is significant. The emotional imprint is the key part to address, even if the exact details are hazy.

Practical Exercise: Timeline of Emotions

Try making a simple timeline of your life, starting from your earliest memory up to the present. Mark any event or stage where you recall strong emotions—good or bad. You might note:

- Age 5: "Moved to a new home. Felt scared."
- Age 8: "Won a small award. Felt proud."
- Age 9: "Got into trouble at school. Felt ashamed."
- Age 12: "Argued with best friend. Felt abandoned."

Notice patterns or repeated feelings. This timeline can help you see where some issues started.

Being Honest Without Self-Judgment

A challenge in recognizing past hurts is judging yourself for how you felt or acted as a child. It might be easy to say, "I was so weak," or "I should have spoken up." But children cannot be expected to handle everything like adults do. Try to see your younger self with understanding.

Why Recognition Aids Healing

Once you recognize your past hurts, you are more likely to stop repeating the old emotional scripts. For instance, if you always felt neglected, you may seek attention in ways that harm you. By naming that hurt, you can seek healthier forms of connection.

What If the Hurt Is Too Overwhelming?

Some memories can be deeply disturbing. If you find yourself feeling panicked, depressed, or unable to function, it may be wise to talk to a mental health professional. Healing is not about forcing yourself to open wounds that are too painful to handle alone. You can go step by step, with guidance if needed.

Real-World Examples of Recognizing Past Hurts

1. **Case of Stress with Authority**:
   - **Situation**: A person feels nervous around bosses or teachers, always expecting harsh criticism.
   - **Possible Childhood Link**: They had a strict teacher in elementary school who punished them for small mistakes.
   - **Result**: As an adult, they interpret any feedback from a boss as a major threat.
   - **Recognition**: By seeing that fear stems from an early memory, they can address it directly, reminding themselves that not all authority figures will punish them.
2. **Case of Avoiding Relationships**:
   - **Situation**: Someone ends every friendship as soon as it gets personal, fearing betrayal.
   - **Possible Childhood Link**: Their parents separated in an unstable way, which left them feeling abandoned.
   - **Result**: They fear the same loss in adult friendships.
   - **Recognition**: Seeing that old fear can help them understand their pattern and work on trusting step by step.
3. **Case of Overly Pleasing Others**:
   - **Situation**: A person agrees to tasks they do not want to do and feels unable to say no.
   - **Possible Childhood Link**: They grew up in a home where they had to keep everyone happy to avoid conflict.
   - **Result**: As an adult, they believe that if they do not comply, people will become angry, and they will be at risk.
   - **Recognition**: Once they see the root cause, they can learn to say no without feeling unsafe.

Possible Emotional Reactions to Recognition

After you recognize a significant childhood hurt, you might experience:

- **Temporary Relief**: You might think, "Now it makes sense! I'm not just irrational."
- **Sadness**: You may grieve for what you lost or never received.
- **Confusion**: You may wonder if you are remembering things correctly.
- **Anger**: You may feel angry at those who caused the hurt, or at yourself for not realizing it sooner.

All these feelings are valid. Allow yourself time and space to process them.

Tips to Stay Balanced

- **Set Boundaries for Your Exploration**: For instance, you might decide to think about past events for only 20 minutes a day. After that, you stop and do something comforting.
- **Use Calm Activities**: Light exercise, coloring, listening to soft music, or spending time in nature can help your mind settle after digging up painful memories.
- **Talk to Supportive People**: Share your thoughts with someone who understands or is at least willing to listen.

How This Sets the Stage for Future Chapters

Recognizing your past hurts is the base for the work in upcoming chapters. You cannot change what you cannot see. Once you shine a light on these hidden or forgotten wounds, you can start to replace negative beliefs with healthier ones. You can also learn how to protect yourself in ways that are based on your current reality, not your childhood fears.

Chapters ahead will show you how to handle emotional responses, practice self-kindness, and set up boundaries. They will also teach you ways to break free from harmful patterns and release unprocessed anger. Think of this chapter as a foundation. It prepares you for deeper emotional work and allows you to face childhood pains that may have seemed locked away.

Summary

- Past hurts can hide in the mind to protect you from pain.
- Signs include unexplained sadness, anger, anxiety, and problems with trust.
- Common childhood hurts include emotional neglect, criticism, and bullying.
- Methods such as journaling, drawing, body scans, and mindful questioning can help uncover hidden hurts.
- Recognition might bring strong emotions, but it is an important step toward healing.
- Memory can be imperfect, but the feelings and beliefs tied to events still matter.
- If the pain feels too overwhelming, seek professional help.
- Understanding your past helps you move forward without staying stuck in old emotional patterns.

CHAPTER 3: BASIC FOUNDATIONS OF EMOTIONAL CARE

Introduction

Many people want to feel calm and steady in their daily lives. However, real peace is not only about external factors, like how much money you have or what job you hold. It also depends on how you handle your emotions. You may have heard the term "emotional care," but might not know exactly what it means. In simple terms, emotional care is the set of habits and tools you use to handle your feelings.

To support your inner child, you need to understand how emotions work, why they can get overwhelming, and what methods can keep you steady. This chapter covers these basics. It shows you practical ways to handle strong feelings so that you can stay balanced, no matter what comes your way.

What Is Emotional Care?

Emotional care is like giving your emotions the same kind of attention you would give a physical wound. If you cut your finger, you clean it and cover it with a bandage. That is physical care. Emotional care works the same way but addresses worries, sadness, anger, or other feelings. You look at your emotions, figure out what they need, and provide the right kind of help.

It might sound simple, but many of us were never taught how to do this. We might have learned to hide our tears or pretend we were fine even if we felt hurt. Emotional care teaches you to be honest about your feelings and treat them kindly.

Why Emotional Care Is Important

1. **Prevents Small Issues From Growing**
   When you ignore your emotions, small hurts can grow bigger. For

example, if you always push down anger, it might build up until it explodes at the wrong time.

2. **Improves Relationships**
   If you know how to care for your emotions, you can also respect others' feelings better. This skill supports healthy bonds with friends, family, and romantic partners.
3. **Boosts Mental Well-Being**
   Consistent emotional care helps you feel more stable. You may worry less and find it easier to cope with life's ups and downs.
4. **Supports the Inner Child**
   When the child part of you feels safe, you experience fewer triggers from old wounds. This can lead to feeling better about who you are right now.

The Link Between Emotions and Thoughts

Emotions and thoughts work together closely. A single event can lead to a thought, which then triggers a feeling. For instance, if you think, "They are ignoring me on purpose," you might feel hurt or angry. If you think, "Maybe they are just busy," you might feel calmer.

Being aware of your thoughts is a key part of emotional care. When your thoughts are harsh or untrue, your emotions can become intense. Learning to notice and adjust your thought patterns is one way to care for your emotional state.

Understanding Basic Emotional Needs

Everyone has a few basic emotional needs:

1. **Safety**: Feeling protected from harm.
2. **Connection**: Feeling close to other people.
3. **Acknowledgment**: Feeling your thoughts and emotions matter.
4. **Respect**: Feeling valued by yourself and by others.

When these needs go unmet, your inner child might protest by causing confusion or distress. You might feel low, anxious, or overly angry. Paying attention to these needs helps you manage many emotional problems before they get out of hand.

Self-Awareness: The Core of Emotional Care

Self-awareness means noticing what you feel and why you feel that way. For many, a big challenge is that feelings show up suddenly, and we act on them without thinking. Self-awareness interrupts this cycle.

Steps to Build Self-Awareness

1. **Pause**: The moment you feel a strong emotion, stop for a second.
2. **Label the Feeling**: Name it: "I feel annoyed," "I feel lonely," or "I feel restless."
3. **Look for the Cause**: Ask yourself, "Why might I feel this way?" The trigger could be a thought or an event.
4. **Check Your Body**: Are you tense in the shoulders? Are you clenching your jaw? Physical cues can provide clues to your emotional state.

By doing these steps often, you form a habit of recognizing emotions quickly.

Emotional Regulation Techniques

Emotional regulation does not mean pushing emotions away. Instead, it means learning how to manage them wisely. Below are a few methods:

1. **Slow Breathing**
    - Inhale to a count of four.
    - Hold for a count of two.
    - Exhale to a count of four.
      Repeat this for at least one minute. This can calm your nervous system.
2. **Relaxing Your Muscles**
    - Start with your toes. Tighten them for five seconds, then relax.
    - Move to your calves, thighs, stomach, arms, shoulders, and so on.
      This method is often called muscle relaxation. It helps release stored tension.

3. **Safe Place Visualization**
   - Think of a simple, real place that felt peaceful to you: maybe a park bench or your bedroom when you were small.
   - Close your eyes and picture the details (colors, shapes, sounds). Spending a minute with this mental image can reduce stress hormones in your body.
4. **Positive Affirmations**
   - Say short, encouraging phrases to yourself: "I can handle this."
   - Keep them simple and direct, so they feel real to you.

Daily Emotional Check-Ins

One powerful habit is to do a quick emotional check-in each day:

- **Morning**: Ask yourself how you feel upon waking. Are you anxious about work? Are you sad for no obvious reason?
- **Midday**: Take a short break to see how your mood has shifted. Maybe you feel relief if the morning tasks are done, or frustration if things did not go as planned.
- **Night**: Notice what feelings you are taking to bed. This helps you spot patterns and address them before they affect your sleep.

This simple practice gives you immediate insight into your emotional rhythms. It makes it less likely for you to be caught off guard by strong feelings.

Speaking Kindly to Yourself

Many people talk to themselves in a harsh way. They might call themselves stupid or lazy. Over time, this can lower your sense of self-worth and make emotional issues worse. Learning to speak kindly to yourself is a key part of emotional care.

Examples of Harsh vs. Kind Self-Talk

- **Harsh**: "I messed up again. I'm useless."
- **Kind**: "I made a mistake, but mistakes happen. I will learn from it."

Changing this internal conversation can feel strange at first, but it helps form a healthier mindset.

Finding Emotional "Hot Buttons"

A "hot button" is an issue or topic that triggers strong emotions. It can be criticism, loud voices, or feeling rejected. When you identify your hot buttons, you can prepare in advance to handle those emotions more calmly.

How to Identify a Hot Button

- **Look at recurring conflicts**: Are you always arguing about the same topics?
- **Notice extreme feelings**: Do you feel rage or panic in certain situations that seem small to others?
- **Recall childhood lessons**: Were there topics in your youth that caused big emotional reactions at home?

By spotting these triggers, you can plan strategies to stay steady when they pop up.

The Power of Emotional Outlets

Suppressing emotions can harm both your mind and body. An emotional outlet is a safe way to let feelings out. Options might include:

- **Writing in a diary**: Spend ten minutes writing whatever comes to mind.
- **Physical activity**: Go for a walk or try some stretches.
- **Talking to a trusted person**: Sharing your thoughts can lessen the emotional load.
- **Artistic projects**: Painting, crafting, or playing music can help release emotional tension.

When you have regular outlets, you reduce the chance of sudden emotional breakdowns.

Avoiding Common Pitfalls in Emotional Care

While learning emotional care, some people make mistakes that block progress:

1. **Believing Emotions Are "Bad"**
   Feelings themselves are not right or wrong; they are signals. Ignoring them prevents you from understanding what they mean.
2. **Wanting to Control All Feelings**
   You cannot control every single emotion. The goal is to guide them in healthy ways, not to switch them off.
3. **Using Unhealthy Coping**
   Some try to manage emotions by overeating, using substances, or hurting themselves. These actions might numb the feelings for a short time but create bigger problems later.
4. **Comparing Your Emotions to Others**
   Each person's emotional world is unique. Telling yourself that you "shouldn't" feel a certain way just because others do not is unhelpful.

Lesser-Known Strategies for Emotional Care (Additional Useful Insights)

1. **Naming Physical Sensations**
   Emotions show up in your body first. Naming bodily sensations—like "my chest feels heavy" or "my stomach is knotted"—can help you pause before your thoughts spiral.
2. **Timed Expression**
   If you find yourself stuck in a negative emotion, give it a set time. For example, allow yourself five minutes to feel frustrated. When the time is up, take action to shift your mindset, like walking or making a simple plan.
3. **Focusing on Values**
   When a strong emotion hits, ask yourself, "What is my most important value right now?" If your value is kindness, for example, this may guide how you respond, even if you are angry.
4. **Emotion Cards**
   Writing emotions on small cards or pieces of paper can help you learn to identify them quickly. For instance, you might have cards labeled "anger,"

"disappointment," "guilt," or "joy." Glance through them when you are unsure how you feel.

Bringing the Inner Child into Emotional Care

Your inner child holds onto old emotional patterns. When you practice emotional care, include that younger part of yourself:

- **Use Child-Friendly Words**: Speak to yourself as if you are talking to a small child. For instance, "It's okay to feel sad," or "You are not in danger."
- **Safe Rituals**: Sometimes, small gestures like hugging a stuffed toy or wrapped blanket can comfort your inner child. This might feel silly, but it can calm deep fears.
- **Reassure Yourself of the Present**: Say, "I am grown now. I can make choices and keep myself safe."

Building Healthy Emotional Routines

Emotional care works best when it is part of your daily life, not just something you do when you are upset. Here are some ideas for regular practice:

1. **Morning Affirmations**
   Choose a short phrase like, "I am capable of handling today." Say it as you start your day.
2. **Lunchtime Mental Break**
   While eating or taking a short break, do a quick body scan. Notice if you are tense. Breathe out stress if you can.
3. **Evening Calm Down**
   Before bed, write a few lines about the day's feelings—both good and bad. This helps you process emotions instead of carrying them into sleep.
4. **Weekend Creativity**
   Reserve at least one hour on the weekend for an activity that frees your mind: drawing, cooking, building something. This playful time allows your inner child to feel engaged and at ease.

Handling Setbacks

No matter how good you get at emotional care, you will still have rough days. Perhaps you find yourself feeling overwhelmed or you forget your calming strategies. That is normal. The path to better emotional health is not a straight line.

When you face a setback:

- **Accept It Happened**: "I got really upset today. That's okay, I'll handle it."
- **Recall Your Tools**: Return to basics: breathing, pausing, writing down thoughts.
- **Learn from the Situation**: Think, "What might have caused this strong reaction?"
- **Try Again**: Emotional care is an ongoing process. Keep practicing.

Real-Life Example of Emotional Care in Action

Case Study:

- **Situation**: Mark feels anxious whenever he is invited to a gathering. He often says no and stays home.
- **Reason**: As a child, Mark's parents argued loudly in social settings, which made him feel unsafe.
- **Emotional Care Steps**:
    1. Mark notices his rapid heartbeat and tense muscles when he gets an invite.
    2. He stops, labels the feeling: "I feel anxious."
    3. He reminds himself he is now an adult, and social events can be safe.
    4. He chooses a simple breathing exercise.
    5. He decides on a small outing with one friend before attending a bigger group event.

By breaking it down, Mark gradually lessens his fear and gains confidence in social situations.

Emotional Care and Your Environment

Sometimes, your environment can block your efforts at emotional care. For example, if you live with people who are always loud or critical, you might find it harder to stay balanced. In such cases:

- **Set Up a Quiet Space**: Even a small corner of a room can serve as a calm zone.
- **Use Headphones**: Listen to soft or neutral sounds that help you relax.
- **Communicate Your Needs**: Tell the people you live with that you need some private time to manage your stress.

If your environment is too toxic, consider making changes when possible. Emotional care might be more effective away from constant negativity.

Myths About Emotional Care

1. **"It's Selfish to Focus on Your Emotions"**
   Caring for your emotions does not mean ignoring others. In fact, being emotionally healthy allows you to support the people around you better.
2. **"Only People With Mental Health Issues Need This"**
   Everyone has emotions. You do not have to be diagnosed with a disorder to need emotional care.
3. **"I'll Become Weak If I Let My Feelings Show"**
   Understanding and naming your feelings actually makes you stronger. It takes courage to be honest about what you feel.
4. **"I Should Always Feel Positive"**
   Being emotionally healthy does not mean you never feel negative. All feelings, including sadness and anger, are normal. The difference is you handle them in safe, healthy ways.

Steps to Strengthen Your Foundation in Emotional Care

- **Commit to Daily Check-Ins**: Even a one-minute pause can build the habit of noticing your feelings.
- **Learn a Few Quick Calming Tools**: Know at least two or three. For example, slow breathing, muscle relaxation, or safe place visualization.
- **Review and Reflect**: Once a week, think about how you handled emotions. Did you avoid them? Did you respond kindly to yourself?
- **Find a Supportive Buddy**: This could be a friend who is also working on emotional health. Share tips and encourage each other.

How This Chapter Connects to the Inner Child

The foundations of emotional care are not just for your adult self. They are also crucial for soothing any old wounds. When you were small, you might not have had the tools to handle strong feelings. Now, as an adult, you can provide those tools. By learning how to calm yourself, you offer relief to that younger part of you that felt helpless or scared in the past.

As you go forward, continue building on these basics. Notice what works well for you and what does not. You do not have to use every single method. Find two or three that fit your lifestyle and personality.

Final Thoughts on Chapter 3

Emotional care is the backbone of healing your inner child. It is about noticing, naming, and handling emotions in a balanced way. When you do this consistently, you create a safer inner environment. This safety can lead to better decisions, healthier relationships, and less emotional turmoil.

In the next chapter, we will look more closely at self-kindness. This is a deeper step, because it focuses on how you speak to and treat yourself every day. If emotional care is about handling feelings, self-kindness is about building a supportive inner dialogue that nurtures both the adult you and the child you once were.

CHAPTER 4: BUILDING SELF-KINDNESS

Introduction

Self-kindness is a way of talking to yourself and treating yourself with understanding. It is linked to self-respect, self-love, and inner safety. Many of us are kinder to strangers or friends than we are to ourselves. This chapter aims to change that pattern by showing you how to develop a habit of treating yourself with patience, warmth, and acceptance.

Building self-kindness is one of the strongest ways to care for your inner child. When you turn this gentle approach inward, you reassure that younger side of you that it is safe to be open and that mistakes do not equal failure. In doing so, you create an internal space where healing can flourish.

The Difference Between Self-Kindness and Self-Pity

Some worry that being kind to themselves might turn into self-pity or making excuses. However, there is a clear difference:

- **Self-Kindness**: Recognizing that everyone has flaws and limits. You treat yourself as you would treat a dear friend who is struggling.
- **Self-Pity**: Feeling sorry for yourself to the point where you believe you cannot do anything about your situation.

In self-kindness, you accept your flaws but do not let them define you. You acknowledge your strengths and weaknesses, then move forward with a gentle mindset. In self-pity, you may focus too heavily on feeling powerless.

Reasons People Struggle With Self-Kindness

1. **Conditioned Criticism**: If you grew up hearing adults say you were not good enough, you might have learned to mirror that self-talk.

2. **Fear of Complacency**: Some believe if they are kind to themselves, they will stop trying to improve.
3. **Guilt**: Others feel they do not deserve kindness if they made past mistakes.
4. **Cultural Pressures**: Some cultures teach you to put yourself last and always focus on others.

By naming these reasons, you can see them for what they are—barriers that keep you from giving yourself the acceptance you need.

Self-Kindness in Action

To become kinder to yourself, try simple steps that reinforce the belief, "I am worthy of care."

1. **Gentle Self-Talk**
    - Replace harsh thoughts with calmer ones.
    - For example, if you think, "I always fail," switch it to, "I have had some rough times, but I can learn to do better."
2. **Writing Gratitude Messages to Yourself**
    - At the end of each day, write down one thing you appreciate about yourself. It could be something minor, like making someone smile, or something big, like finishing a difficult task.
3. **Allowing Small Pleasures**
    - Give yourself the chance to enjoy small moments: a warm shower, a cozy blanket, or a favorite snack. Recognize these little joys as signs that you matter.
4. **Speaking Up for Your Needs**
    - If someone is crossing your boundaries, let them know (politely but firmly). Self-kindness includes protecting your emotional space.

Addressing Negative Core Beliefs

Negative core beliefs are the deep ideas you hold about yourself, such as "I am not worthy" or "I cannot do anything right." They often stem from hurtful childhood messages.

How to Challenge Negative Core Beliefs

1. **Notice the Thought**: The moment you catch yourself thinking, "I'm useless," label it as a belief, not a fact.
2. **Look for Proof**: Ask, "Is there proof I am useless?" or "Do I have examples of doing well in life?"
3. **Replace With Balanced Thoughts**: For instance, "I have made mistakes, but I have also achieved many things."
4. **Practice Repetition**: Each time the negative belief returns, challenge it again. Over time, this weakens its hold.

Self-Kindness and Mistakes

Many people attack themselves when they make a mistake. Yet, mistakes are natural. They can help you learn. Here is how you can respond with self-kindness when something goes wrong:

1. **Pause**: Take a breath.
2. **Acknowledge the Error**: "I made a mistake."
3. **Self-Kindness Phrase**: "I am still a good person who can grow."
4. **Plan to Correct**: "Next time, I'll try a different approach."

This process helps you face errors without turning them into personal attacks on your worth.

The Inner Child and Self-Kindness

A child often expects adults to offer warmth and comfort. If this did not happen in your childhood, you might have grown up thinking, "I must not be lovable." By practicing self-kindness, you counter that old idea.

- **Picture Your Younger Self**: Imagine yourself at a young age. Would you want to say harsh things to that child? Probably not.
- **Offer Reassurance**: Say, "It is okay. You are trying your best," or "You deserve care and love."

- **Small Acts of Fun**: Let the child part of you feel lightness. This might be watching a funny cartoon, scribbling with crayons, or playing with a small toy for a few moments.

Traps That Block Self-Kindness

1. **Perfectionism**: Believing you must be perfect to be okay. This mind-set leaves no room for mistakes or growth.
2. **Over-Apologizing**: Apologizing for things that are not your responsibility. It can be a sign you think you are always at fault.
3. **Shutting Down Praise**: When someone compliments you, do you brush it off or disagree? That can signal trouble accepting kindness.
4. **Comparing Pain**: Telling yourself, "Others have it worse, so I should not feel bad." This denies your own feelings.

Recognizing these traps helps you step away from them and move toward a friendlier stance toward yourself.

Practical Exercises for Self-Kindness

Exercise 1: The Mirror Technique

1. Stand in front of a mirror.
2. Look yourself in the eyes for a few seconds.
3. Say something supportive out loud, such as, "You matter. You are growing every day."
4. If it feels awkward, notice the discomfort and keep going. With practice, it becomes easier.

Exercise 2: The "Thank You" Note

1. Take a piece of paper.
2. Write "Dear Me, Thank you for..."
3. List at least three things you are thankful to yourself for doing, such as finishing a task, being patient with someone, or sticking to a personal goal.

4. Read your note back to yourself.

Exercise 3: Acceptance vs. Approval

1. Think of something you do not like about yourself.
2. Write down why this trait or behavior bothers you.
3. Now, separate acceptance from approval:
   - Acceptance means you see it for what it is, without denial.
   - Approval would mean you fully support it. Sometimes, you might not approve of your own habits, but you can still accept that they exist.
4. A short phrase: "I see that I tend to be forgetful, and I accept it is part of me right now." By accepting it, you reduce self-judgment and gain the clarity to improve if you choose.

Self-Kindness and Boundaries

Kindness to yourself includes respecting your emotional and physical limits. If you let others drain you because you are scared to say no, that is not self-kindness.

Examples of Healthy Boundaries

- Saying "no" to extra tasks if you are already overwhelmed.
- Telling a friend you need a moment alone if you feel anxious or tired.
- Keeping your personal information private when you do not feel safe sharing it.

When you respect these limits, you show your inner child that it is cared for.

Changing Your Inner Dialog

Sometimes, the way we speak to ourselves is learned from caregivers or environment. To become kinder inside, you might need to replace old scripts:

- **Old Script**: "Why can't I get this right? I'm so bad at this."
- **New Script**: "I'm trying something new. It's normal to struggle a bit."

This change takes time, but each small shift helps create a more nurturing tone inside your mind.

Lesser-Known Approaches to Strengthen Self-Kindness (Extra Useful Insights)

1. **Kindness Triggers**
    - Pick an item you see often: a bracelet, a keychain, or a small sticker on your phone.
    - Each time you see it, say one kind thing to yourself. This trains your brain to link that object with a friendly inner voice.
2. **Name the Kind Voice**
    - Some people find it helpful to give a name to their kind inner voice, like "Coach Sam" or "Supportive Jess."
    - When you hear negativity in your mind, mentally call on that named voice to speak. It sounds a bit playful, but it can help you shift your mindset quickly.
3. **Reviewing Success Journals**
    - Keep a small notebook of successes—big or small. Write down every personal win or time you overcame a challenge.
    - On hard days, review those entries to remind yourself you do have skills and strength.
4. **Light Physical Comfort**
    - A gentle hand on your chest or a slight self-hug can activate calming responses in the body. This can be surprisingly soothing, especially if you lacked physical comfort in childhood.

Real-World Stories of Self-Kindness

1. **Case of Overwork**
    - **Situation**: Sarah works 10-hour days and feels guilty if she rests.
    - **Underlying Reason**: She grew up in a home where her parents called her lazy if she took a break.
    - **Self-Kindness Practice**: Sarah plans a 15-minute break every two hours at work. During that break, she tells herself, "Rest is allowed.

I'm not lazy." Over time, she learns that rest helps her be more productive and less stressed.

2. **Case of Social Anxiety**
   - **Situation**: Ben feels awkward in social settings and thinks, "I'm weird. People must think I'm stupid."
   - **Underlying Reason**: He was teased as a child for being shy.
   - **Self-Kindness Practice**: Ben writes down supportive phrases like, "Some people are quiet and that's fine," "I add value by listening well." He reads these before social events. This helps him feel calmer and more confident.
3. **Case of Childhood Neglect**
   - **Situation**: Maria grew up with parents who were never around. She believes she is not interesting enough for people to stay.
   - **Self-Kindness Practice**: Maria starts a daily note to herself: "I am worthy of good friendships." She also allows herself short moments of fun each day—like doodling or listening to music—reminding herself that she deserves enjoyment. Gradually, she feels less fear about being left out.

Facing Resistance to Self-Kindness

It is common to feel uneasy when trying to be kind to yourself, especially if you have been harsh for a long time. You might think, "This is silly," or "I do not deserve it." Recognize that feeling as a leftover pattern from past experiences. You can allow the thought to arise without letting it stop you.

Keep doing small acts of kindness toward yourself. Over time, your mind starts to see them as normal. If needed, share your feelings with a counselor or a trusted friend. Let them know you are working on being less critical of yourself.

How Self-Kindness Affects Others

Ironically, being kind to yourself often leads to you being kinder to those around you. When you stop judging yourself so harshly, you also become less critical of other people. This shift can improve your relationships at home and at work. You might even notice that friends or family become more open, because they sense you are in a calmer emotional state.

Connecting Self-Kindness with Future Growth

Self-kindness does not mean you stay stuck. Instead, it can be a stepping stone to progress. When you see yourself in a gentle light, you are more likely to try new things, since you are not overwhelmed by fear of failure. You become more open to feedback because you know a setback does not define your worth.

Daily Habits to Grow Self-Kindness

Below are practical ways to make self-kindness a regular part of your life:

1. **Morning Self-Check**
   - Upon waking, ask, "How do I feel physically and mentally?"
   - If you notice stress, say a gentle phrase to yourself or do a short breathing exercise.
2. **Gentle Emails or Texts**
   - Send a kind message to yourself. Yes, it may sound odd, but writing a short friendly text to your own phone or an email to your inbox with a positive note can create a small boost.
3. **Short Relaxation Breaks**
   - Set a timer for two or three short breaks in the day. During these breaks, close your eyes, breathe, or listen to a calming tune. Focus on the idea that you deserve this break.
4. **Praise Tracking**
   - Make a list of any compliments you receive or positive feedback. Revisit this list when you doubt yourself.

Overcoming Guilt and Shame With Self-Kindness

Guilt can occur when you think you have done something wrong. Shame can occur when you believe you are flawed at your core. Both guilt and shame can stand in the way of being kind to yourself.

To handle guilt, see if there is a real action to correct. If so, do what you can: apologize, fix the mistake, or make amends. After that, allow yourself to move forward.

To handle shame, remember that who you are is not defined by a single behavior or shortcoming. Each person is more than any one event or trait. Self-kindness involves acknowledging that truth.

How This Chapter Prepares You for Future Topics

Learning self-kindness sets the stage for stronger self-trust, better boundary-setting, and healthier coping with shame or fear. In the next chapters, you will explore ways to break harmful patterns and build safe relationships. All these steps will be easier if you already see yourself as someone worthy of a gentle and understanding approach.

Consider this chapter as a tool kit. You might not use every suggestion right away, but knowing they exist can guide you when you face tough times. With each small act of self-kindness, you teach your inner child that the world can be a more caring place—starting with how you treat yourself.

Summary of Key Points in Chapter 4

- **Self-kindness is an approach that recognizes you are human and worthy of support.**
- **It is not the same as self-pity, which can lead to feeling helpless.**
- **Past childhood messages may block self-kindness, but you can replace them with more helpful thoughts.**
- **Use simple steps: gentle self-talk, gratitude messages to yourself, and standing firm on personal boundaries.**
- **Self-kindness supports the inner child by creating a sense of warmth and safety.**
- **This approach helps you handle mistakes, guilt, and shame in a more balanced way.**
- **Over time, being kinder to yourself leads to treating others with more kindness as well.**

CHAPTER 5: TRUSTING YOUR OWN THOUGHTS

Introduction

Many people go through life feeling uncertain about their decisions and viewpoints. They might worry that their thoughts are not valid or that they cannot trust their own mind. This doubt can become stronger if a person's caregivers or peers brushed aside their opinions when they were young. Feeling that your thoughts do not matter can stay with you into adulthood, causing second-guessing and confusion.

In this chapter, we will discuss why trusting your own thoughts is a core part of emotional well-being. We will look at how childhood experiences might have led you to doubt yourself and how to shift that pattern. You will find practical tips for forming a healthier relationship with your own mind. By the end, you should feel more confident that your thoughts are worth hearing—both by yourself and by others.

Why We Doubt Our Thoughts

1. **Early Disapproval**: If, as a child, you shared an idea or feeling only to be ignored or scolded, you might have learned not to trust your own ideas. Over time, this can show up as a habit of always checking with others before making a decision.
2. **Harsh Self-Talk**: Sometimes, we repeat negative messages we heard when we were small. This can sound like, "You're not smart enough," or "Your opinions are silly." These messages might replay in your mind, blocking your confidence.
3. **Fear of Conflict**: If, in the past, disagreeing with someone led to arguments or punishment, you might avoid stating your thoughts to keep the peace. Eventually, you could lose touch with your true opinions.
4. **Social Pressures**: Modern life can be fast and filled with strong opinions. If everyone around you seems certain, you may feel hesitant to trust yourself, especially if you grew up feeling your voice was less important.

The Value of Trusting Your Own Thoughts

1. **Healthy Boundaries**: When you trust your thoughts, you know where you stand on issues. This helps you set limits and let others know how you feel.
2. **Better Decisions**: If you are always unsure, you might rely too much on external advice. But external advice can sometimes be wrong for you. By trusting yourself, you can make decisions aligned with your core values.
3. **Higher Self-Esteem**: Recognizing that your thoughts matter boosts your sense of self-worth.
4. **Less Regret**: People who ignore their own instincts can end up regretting their choices. Trusting yourself reduces the chance of feeling forced into situations that do not fit you.

Recognizing When You Are Distrusting Your Own Thoughts

Sometimes, self-doubt is so normal that you might not even realize it is happening. Here are common signs:

- **Constantly Seeking Confirmation**: You keep asking others, "Is this right?" even when it is something you know well.
- **Difficulty Making Simple Choices**: You find it stressful to decide what to eat, how to dress, or which movie to watch.
- **Overthinking**: You replay the same scenario in your mind countless times, afraid to settle on a conclusion.
- **Emotional Discomfort**: You feel a nagging sense that your true thoughts are being silenced, leading to tension or sadness.

When these signs appear, it can mean you do not fully trust your own viewpoint.

Overcoming the Fear of Being Wrong

A big reason people do not trust themselves is the fear of being incorrect. No one wants to be mocked or told, "I told you so." Yet, being wrong is part of the human experience. The question is not whether you will make a mistake, but how you deal with it once it happens.

1. **Accept That Mistakes Happen**: Everyone makes errors at some point. Recognizing this helps reduce the fear that being wrong means you are worthless.
2. **Learn from Errors**: Each time you make a decision that does not work out, ask, “What can I learn here?” or “How can I approach this differently next time?”
3. **Focus on Growth Instead of Perfection**: If you see each choice as an experiment, you reduce the stress around being 100% correct all the time.

Differentiating Between Self-Doubt and Reasonable Concern

It is healthy to think carefully before taking action, especially in serious matters like finances, health, or relationships. Taking a moment to consider risks or gather more information is wise. But there is a difference between thoughtful caution and a lack of trust in your own mind.

- **Thoughtful Caution**: “Let me research the pros and cons of this plan before deciding.”
- **Chronic Self-Doubt**: “I probably can’t make good decisions anyway, so I won’t even bother thinking it through.”

Learning to tell these apart can help you know when you are being wisely cautious versus when you are stuck in self-doubt.

Steps to Strengthen Trust in Your Own Thoughts

Step 1: Awareness of Negative Self-Talk

First, pay attention to any mental phrases that put you down. For example:

- “I’m not good at this.”
- “Nobody cares what I think.”
- “I need someone else to confirm.”

When you catch such phrases, note them in a small notebook or a phone app. This will help you see patterns.

Step 2: Question the Doubt

Once you identify a negative statement, ask yourself:

- "Is this always true?"
- "Who told me this originally?"
- "Do I have any evidence that contradicts this statement?"

Often, you will realize your negative thought is an old message, not a proven fact.

Step 3: Collect Small Wins

Write down times when trusting your own thoughts led to a good outcome. It does not have to be huge. Maybe you chose a specific route to work and avoided traffic, or you offered a suggestion in a meeting and it was well-received. These small examples build confidence.

Step 4: Take Calculated Risks

Try trusting your opinion in low-stakes situations. For instance, pick a restaurant without asking others, or choose a weekend activity based on your personal interests. As you see positive outcomes, your self-trust will grow.

Step 5: Reflect on Experiences

At the end of the day, review moments when you followed your own thoughts. Ask: "How did it feel?" "What went well?" "What can I improve next time?" Reflection helps you build self-awareness and refine your decision-making process.

Practical Exercises to Strengthen Self-Trust

Exercise 1: Thought Validation

1. Pick a small decision you need to make (such as what to cook for dinner).
2. Write down your initial opinion without asking anyone.

3. List any doubts that come up. For example: "I might mess up the recipe." "No one will like what I choose."
4. Write a counter-argument to each doubt, such as: "I can pick a simple meal." "Everyone has different tastes, but it's fine to try."
5. Make your choice based on your own thinking. Notice how it feels to rely on yourself.

Exercise 2: Reclaiming Past Choices

1. Think of three decisions you made in the past that turned out well.
2. Write a short sentence on how you reached each decision: "I listened to my gut," or "I gathered facts and trusted my conclusion."
3. Notice any common strengths in your approach. This can remind you of how capable you are when you allow yourself to think freely.

Exercise 3: The "Voice in the Crowd" Method

1. Imagine you are in a room filled with many voices giving you conflicting advice.
2. In your mind, turn down the volume of those other voices.
3. Let your own voice speak clearly and see what it says. This is a mental trick to find your genuine opinion when external pressures are overwhelming.

The Inner Child's Role in Self-Trust

When you were small, you might have formed beliefs about whether your opinions mattered. If adults ignored or belittled you, your inner child might still be stuck in a mindset of "I have nothing important to say."

To help that younger side of you:

- **Visualize**: Picture yourself as a child, trying to share an idea. In your mind, respond with warmth: "I hear you. Your thoughts make sense."
- **Practice Safety**: Remind yourself that, as an adult, you have the right to think freely without punishment.
- **Encourage Curiosity**: Children naturally explore and share thoughts. Try to reconnect with that curiosity and freedom.

When Others Disagree With Your Thoughts

Even if you trust your own mind, others might not always agree with you. This does not mean you are wrong. People come from different backgrounds and have diverse views. Here are ways to handle disagreements:

1. **Stay Calm**: Take a breath. Disagreement is normal.
2. **Ask Questions**: Try to understand the other person's viewpoint without immediately giving up your own.
3. **Explain Your Reasons**: Share how you arrived at your thought or opinion.
4. **Decide Whether to Adjust or Hold Firm**: If the other person raises a good point, you can adjust your stance. If not, you can keep your original view.

Not every disagreement has to be tense. Sometimes, it can be an opening to learn, or at least to respect different perspectives.

Handling Criticism

Criticism can shake your trust in your own thoughts if you take it personally. However, criticism might also hold useful insights. The key is to separate constructive feedback from unhelpful attacks.

- **Constructive Feedback**: Points out areas where you can grow. Example: "I see you made a strong start, but maybe you can add more detail in the middle."
- **Unhelpful Attacks**: Attacks you as a person without offering solutions. Example: "You always mess up. You have no idea what you're doing."

When you receive constructive feedback, you can choose to integrate the helpful part. When faced with unhelpful attacks, remind yourself that the critic is not offering real guidance. You can take a moment to reaffirm your own thought process.

Trusting Intuition vs. Overthinking

Sometimes, your mind gives you a gut feeling about a situation. This is often called intuition. Intuition can be shaped by past knowledge, experiences, and cues you pick up without realizing it. Overthinking, on the other hand, might cause you to miss the simpler truths in front of you.

- **When to Trust Intuition**: If the decision matches with known facts and there is no immediate danger in following that feeling, it might be worth trusting.
- **When to Slow Down**: If your intuition leads to constant worry or if the stakes are very high (like signing a big contract), it could be wise to do extra research.

Balancing gut instincts with logical thinking is a skill that grows as you practice trusting your own mind.

Real-Life Examples of Building Self-Trust

1. **Lena's New Job Offer**
    - **Situation**: Lena received a job offer but doubted her ability to succeed in a new field.
    - **Past Influence**: As a child, her parents often called her choices "reckless."
    - **Action**: Lena wrote down her skills, compared them to the job requirements, and realized she was actually qualified.
    - **Outcome**: She took the job, discovered she could learn quickly, and felt more confident in her problem-solving.
2. **Dario's Creative Project**
    - **Situation**: Dario wanted to start a small art project, but he feared people would think it was strange.
    - **Past Influence**: In school, his teacher once mocked his drawing style.
    - **Action**: Dario picked one piece of art he felt proud of and shared it with a supportive friend. The friend responded positively, giving Dario a boost.
    - **Outcome**: He continued the project, realized others found his art interesting, and gained faith in his creative thoughts.

3. **Asha's Family Conflict**
    - **Situation**: Asha's relatives often overruled her suggestions during gatherings.
    - **Past Influence**: She grew up in a loud household where her voice was drowned out.
    - **Action**: Asha practiced saying, "I would like to contribute an idea," in a calm but firm tone. She reminded herself that her viewpoint was valid.
    - **Outcome**: Over time, her relatives realized she could offer good ideas. Asha felt more secure expressing herself, even if her suggestions did not always win.

Lesser-Known Insights on Self-Trust (Extra Useful Information)

1. **Body Clues**
   Sometimes, your body reacts before your mind fully processes a thought. You may feel tightness in your chest, warmth in your cheeks, or a tingle in your stomach. Paying attention to these body signals can help you sense if you are uneasy or aligned with your own idea.
2. **Short Breathing Check**
   If you notice shallow breathing when you consider an opinion, it could mean anxiety is blocking your self-trust. A quick full inhale and slow exhale might clear your head to think more honestly.
3. **Naming the Critic**
   If you have a strong internal critic that constantly undermines you, give it a label. For instance, call it "The Disapprover." When the negative voice appears, you can say, "That's just The Disapprover talking again," to keep it separate from your true self.
4. **Memo to Yourself**
   Write a memo (short note) to your future self that says, "You have made thoughtful decisions before. You are allowed to speak your mind." Read it when you feel uncertain.

Balancing Advice From Others With Your Own Thoughts

It is healthy to gather input from trusted friends or mentors. However, too much external advice can drown out your own voice. The goal is to find a balance.

- **Ask for Specifics**: Instead of a general "What do you think I should do?" ask, "Can you suggest some pros and cons?" This way, you get information but still decide on your own.
- **Respect Your Feelings**: If someone's advice goes against your instincts in a major way, pause and ask yourself why. Your hesitation might reveal something important.
- **Take a Break**: Step away from the conversation and spend time alone to process the advice. Then see if your thoughts match or differ.

Moving From Second-Guessing to Confidence

Learning to trust your own thoughts is similar to building a muscle. The more you use it, the stronger it gets. At first, you might feel shaky, but each time you successfully follow your own reasoning, you reinforce a sense of self-reliance.

- **Celebrate Small Victories**: If you made a decision to attend a new class and it turned out well, acknowledge it. A short statement like, "My own thought led me here, and it worked," can do wonders for your confidence.
- **No Need to Boast**: Trusting your own mind does not mean putting others down or ignoring outside help. It is simply recognizing that your viewpoint matters too.
- **Mistakes Are Part of Growth**: If you make a choice that fails, it does not mean you were foolish to trust yourself. It just means you learned something new.

How Trusting Your Own Thoughts Impacts the Inner Child for Good

Each time you show trust in your own ideas, you send a message to your inner child: "We are allowed to have opinions and make decisions. We are not helpless." This can help undo old beliefs of powerlessness. Over time, your inner child may feel less need to hide or seek constant approval. This sense of mental safety can reduce anxiety and foster a more positive self-image.

Dealing With Setbacks on the Path to Self-Trust

Even after learning these methods, you might slip back into doubt. Perhaps a harsh comment from a friend or a stressful week at work causes you to question yourself again. When that happens:

1. **Pause**: Remind yourself that setbacks are normal.
2. **Revisit Helpful Methods**: Look at your list of previous successes. Practice a short breathing exercise.
3. **Speak Kindly to Yourself**: Instead of saying, "I knew I couldn't trust myself," say, "I'm having a tough moment, but I can handle it."
4. **Plan a Small Action**: Regain momentum by making and trusting one simple choice, like picking a meal or scheduling a personal activity.

Conclusion of Chapter 5

Trusting your own thoughts is a process that involves breaking old patterns, challenging negative beliefs, and learning from both successes and mistakes. This trust grows as you acknowledge that your opinions are valid, even if they differ from others. For many people, the biggest shift occurs when they realize that being wrong sometimes does not make them unworthy.

As you continue to practice self-trust, you will likely see improvements in decision-making, relationships, and overall peace of mind. Your inner child will benefit too, as it learns it is safe to speak and think without being ignored or punished.

In the next chapter, we will explore how to break harmful patterns that may have started long ago. While trusting your own thoughts is a key part of growth, it often goes hand-in-hand with letting go of old habits that cause emotional damage. You will learn to spot these patterns and replace them with healthier ways of thinking and acting.

CHAPTER 6: BREAKING HARMFUL PATTERNS

Introduction

We all develop patterns in life—ways of thinking, feeling, and behaving that repeat over time. Sometimes, these patterns are helpful, such as brushing your teeth each morning or showing politeness to others. Other times, they are harmful, like constant self-criticism, people-pleasing, or avoiding problems until they explode. These harmful patterns can be linked to childhood experiences or messages we absorbed when we were too young to know better.

This chapter focuses on identifying your harmful patterns, understanding why they formed, and learning practical strategies to replace them. When you break free of these ingrained routines, you pave the way for deeper healing. This includes supporting your inner child, who may still be stuck in a state of fear or shame if old patterns remain unchallenged.

Understanding What a Pattern Is

A pattern is a repeated chain of thoughts and actions in response to certain triggers. For example:

- **Trigger**: You feel lonely.
- **Pattern**: You call someone who often manipulates you because you fear being alone.
- **Outcome**: You end up feeling drained or anxious, which confirms your negative view of yourself.

Over time, your brain can default to this pattern so often that you no longer question it. Recognizing that you are stuck in a loop is the first step toward change.

Why Harmful Patterns Persist

1. **Familiarity**: Even if something causes pain, it can feel comfortable in a strange way if you have always done it.
2. **Lack of Awareness**: Some patterns started so early in life that you might not realize there is another way.
3. **Emotional Payoff**: Certain negative behaviors might bring short-term relief, like overindulging in snacks or escaping into video games, even if they hurt you later.
4. **Fear of Change**: Breaking a pattern can be scary because it forces you to face the unknown.

Examples of Harmful Patterns

- **Passive-Aggressive Communication**: Instead of saying what upsets you, you withdraw or use sharp remarks that hint at anger.
- **Rejecting Compliments**: You wave off any praise, reinforcing the idea that you are not good enough.
- **Needing Approval**: You constantly look for people to confirm your worth, which can be exhausting for both you and them.
- **Overworking**: You bury yourself in tasks to avoid dealing with emotional problems.
- **Sudden Anger**: You hold in frustrations until they burst out in a moment of rage.

Identifying Your Own Harmful Patterns

1. Keep a Behavior Log

For one week, note situations where you felt strong emotions. Write down what you did, what you felt, and the result. You might see the same behavior repeated across different days.

2. Ask for Honest Feedback

If you have a trusted friend or counselor, ask them gently, "Have you noticed any habits in me that seem harmful?" You may learn about patterns you are blind to.

3. Review Your Childhood

Think about how your family handled stress or conflict. Did they shout, give silent treatment, or blame one another? Sometimes, you may carry similar tactics into your adult life without realizing it.

4. Notice the Outcome

If you see that a certain action always ends in guilt, fear, or strained relationships, that is a sign of a harmful pattern.

The Link to Your Inner Child

Often, harmful patterns started as coping methods when you were small. For instance, if you had to keep quiet to avoid punishment, you might have learned to ignore your needs or opinions. As an adult, you might follow the same pattern, remaining silent or agreeable even when it hurts you.

By breaking these patterns, you show your inner child that survival modes from the past are no longer needed. You can replace them with healthier methods that fit your current life situation.

Steps to Break Harmful Patterns

Step 1: Awareness and Honesty

Admit to yourself that a certain behavior is not serving you. This can be hard because it often involves facing uncomfortable truths. You might think, "I avoid serious talks with my partner and then blow up in anger later." Being real about this habit is a major leap forward.

Step 2: Understand the Trigger

Notice what sets off the pattern. Is it stress, fear of being alone, feeling disrespected, or financial worry? Identifying triggers helps you prepare.

Step 3: Pause Before Acting

When you sense a trigger, take a moment to breathe or count to ten. This brief break can stop the automatic cycle of harmful behavior, giving you a chance to choose a different response.

Step 4: Replace the Pattern

Do not just try to stop the behavior; replace it with a healthier action. For example, instead of reaching for junk food when you are upset, you could try journaling or taking a brief walk.

Step 5: Repeat

Behavior change takes consistent practice. Expect slip-ups but keep trying. The more you practice, the easier the new pattern becomes.

Dealing With Emotional Pain During the Process

Changing an old pattern can bring up sadness, anger, or fear. After all, it has been part of you for a long time. Here are ways to handle these emotions:

- **Acceptance of Feelings**: Say to yourself, "It is normal to feel unsettled when trying something new."
- **Self-Kindness**: Treat yourself with warmth. If you slip, do not call yourself a failure. Instead, see it as another opportunity to learn.
- **Support System**: Let supportive friends or a counselor know you are in the process of change. They can provide encouragement.

Practical Methods to Break Patterns

Method 1: The "Stop and Question" Approach

1. When a trigger occurs, say "Stop" in your mind.
2. Ask yourself, "What do I normally do in this situation?"
3. Ask, "How do I usually feel afterward?"
4. Decide on a different, healthier action.

By turning off the autopilot response, you increase your chances of responding in a new way.

Method 2: A Daily Habit Tracker

1. Identify one pattern you want to change, such as snapping at family members when stressed.
2. Each day, place a check mark on your habit tracker if you successfully manage your stress in a better way. If not, mark an X.
3. At the end of the week, review your progress. Celebrate each check mark as proof you can change, and note what might have caused the X's so you can prepare better next time.

(Note: Use a word like "recognize" or "note" your successes, rather than a word you asked not to use.)

Method 3: Create a "Safe Script"

1. Write out what you would like to say or do instead of following your harmful pattern.
2. For example, if your pattern is to yell when you feel ignored, a safe script might be: "I feel upset and would like to talk about it calmly."
3. Practice this script in your mind (or out loud) when you are calm, so it is easier to use when the trigger actually happens.

Avoiding the Trap of Self-Blame

When people realize they have a harmful pattern, they sometimes feel ashamed or guilty. They might say, "It's all my fault I'm this way." But remember, you picked up these patterns at a time when you were likely too young to see other options. Or you learned them to cope with a situation bigger than you could handle. Blaming yourself keeps you stuck. Aim for understanding instead of self-punishment.

Real-Life Examples of Breaking Harmful Patterns

1. **Case: Jade and the Guilt Cycle**
   - **Harmful Pattern**: Jade says yes to everyone's requests, then feels exhausted and resentful.
   - **Trigger**: Feeling obligated whenever someone asks for help.
   - **Replacement Action**: Jade practices pausing before saying yes. She tells the person, "Let me check my schedule." This gives her time to think about whether she can or wants to help.
   - **Outcome**: Over time, she learns to say no politely, protecting her energy and reducing guilt.
2. **Case: Ron and Avoidance**
   - **Harmful Pattern**: Ron delays paying bills until the last second, leading to late fees.
   - **Trigger**: Anxiety over looking at his finances.
   - **Replacement Action**: Ron sets up a weekly financial check-in on a calendar. He challenges himself to open bills as soon as they arrive.
   - **Outcome**: Although he feels nervous at first, the routine helps him stay on track and avoid the stressful cycle of last-minute scrambling.
3. **Case: Billie and Angry Outbursts**
   - **Harmful Pattern**: Billie yells at family members when under stress.
   - **Trigger**: Overwork, feeling that no one listens.
   - **Replacement Action**: Billie takes a break to breathe and uses a calm statement: "I'm feeling edgy and need a minute."
   - **Outcome**: Fewer shouting matches, and family members become more understanding when Billie needs space to cool down.

Ways to Make New Patterns Stick

1. **Start Small**: Pick one pattern to focus on at a time. Trying to change everything at once can overwhelm you.
2. **Reward Progress**: Each time you follow your replacement action instead of the harmful one, treat yourself to something simple—like a short relaxing pause or a small note of praise.
3. **Be Patient**: Patterns formed over years do not vanish overnight. Consistency is key.

4. **Track Changes Over Time**: Write down your progress weekly. Notice even small improvements.

The Role of Forgiveness in Breaking Patterns

You might need to forgive yourself for the ways you once behaved. This does not excuse hurtful actions but recognizes that you may have acted out of fear or learned habits. Self-forgiveness frees you from the weight of shame, letting you move forward with a clear mind.

Additionally, if others were involved (like caregivers or siblings), you may face the choice of forgiving them, too. This does not mean forgetting or approving what happened. It just means releasing the hold it has on you so you can build healthier behaviors now.

What If the Pattern Involves Others?

Some harmful patterns are not just about how you behave; they also involve how you interact with certain people who encourage or expect that behavior. If your pattern is tied to a toxic relationship, you may need to set boundaries or limit contact. Change is harder if those around you keep you stuck.

- **Be Clear About Your Intentions**: Let the other person know you are trying to change. For example, "I'm working on not losing my temper. I might step away if I feel we're getting too heated."
- **Seek Mutual Respect**: If the other person does not respect your wish to break the pattern, you may need to reduce their influence on your life where possible.
- **Consider Professional Help**: Couples or family counseling can help if the harmful pattern involves multiple people.

Breaking Patterns Tied to Trauma

Some patterns are rooted in deep traumas, such as abuse or major loss. If that is the case, you may feel strong fear or pain when you try to change. Professional therapy can be a valuable tool here. A therapist can guide you through the process in a safe setting, ensuring you do not become overwhelmed.

Hidden Patterns: When Behavior Is Subtle

Not all harmful patterns are obvious. Sometimes, they appear in small ways that add up over time. Examples:

- **Self-Insults**: You quietly call yourself names in your head each time something goes wrong.
- **Agreeing Without Checking In**: You nod and say yes just to avoid tension, even if you have no plan or desire to follow through.
- **Saying "It's Fine" When It's Not**: Minimizing your own feelings can create bottled-up emotions that eventually spill out.

Pay attention to these subtle patterns. They can be just as harmful as big, dramatic ones.

Additional Insights (Extra Useful Information)

1. **Future Vision**
   Sometimes imagining a future where you are free from the old pattern can motivate you. For instance, if you often avoid conflict, picture yourself calmly stating your needs and feeling proud afterward.
2. **Anchoring Technique**
   People sometimes use a physical touch (like pressing two fingers together) as a signal to switch to the new behavior. It creates a small but helpful link in the brain that says, "Remember to change course now."
3. **Mindful Movement**
   Engaging in slow, focused movement (like certain light stretches) can help bring your attention to the present moment, breaking mental loops that fuel old habits.

4. **Scripting for Tough Moments**
   Writing short scripts for tricky social encounters can be very helpful. For example, if your pattern is to get defensive when teased, prepare a gentle but firm reply: "I don't find that funny. Let's change the topic." This practice keeps you from falling into the old reaction of either laughing it off or exploding.

Monitoring Success and Adjusting

Breaking harmful patterns is not a one-step process. As you move forward, you may discover new triggers, or realize the pattern goes deeper than you first thought. That is okay. You can adjust your approach anytime.

- **Regular Check-Ins**: Every couple of weeks, see how you are doing with the new behavior.
- **Adaptation**: If a replacement action stops working, brainstorm another one.
- **Progress, Not Perfection**: Aim for gradual change. Even a partial improvement is a step in the right direction.

How Breaking Patterns Helps Your Inner Child

When you adopt healthier behaviors, you become a more dependable caretaker for the younger side of you. Your inner child may feel relief, realizing that the chaos or fear from old patterns no longer runs the show. This can bring a sense of stability and trust, which is essential for ongoing emotional healing.

Common Pitfalls and How to Avoid Them

1. **Trying to Fix Everything at Once**: Focus on one pattern at a time to avoid burnout.
2. **Hiding Setbacks**: Feeling ashamed can make you hide slip-ups. Instead, admit them openly so you can learn.

3. **Ignoring Emotional Needs**: If the pattern was originally a coping method for stress or fear, you must address those deeper feelings or the pattern may return.
4. **Refusing Help**: Sometimes, help from a trusted friend, support group, or therapist is needed for deeper patterns.

Conclusion of Chapter 6

Breaking harmful patterns is a key step in healing your inner child and improving your emotional life. While these patterns may have started long ago, you now have the power to change them. By identifying triggers, pausing before reacting, and replacing old habits with healthier ones, you reclaim control.

Yes, this process can be challenging, and setbacks will happen. But each time you catch the old pattern and choose something better, you plant a seed of change that can grow over time. You also show that younger part of yourself that a different way of living exists—one that is safer, kinder, and more in tune with your true values.

In the upcoming chapters, we will explore more techniques for improving your emotional health and building stronger connections with others. This includes boundary-setting, overcoming shame, and forming healthy networks of support. The work you have done in trusting your own thoughts and breaking patterns will serve as a solid foundation for all these new insights.

CHAPTER 7: HEALTHY BOUNDARIES

Introduction

A boundary is like an invisible line that marks where your personal comfort and limits end and where another person's space begins. It shows people how to treat you and lets them know what you can and cannot accept. Boundaries are not just about telling others "no"; they also guide how you let yourself be treated in many parts of life—emotional, physical, mental, and digital.

When you set a boundary, you are letting the world know your needs and limits matter. For many, boundaries can feel confusing if they grew up in homes where personal space was not respected or if their opinions were often ignored. In this chapter, we will break down the idea of healthy boundaries, explain how they connect to your inner child, and offer steps to build and maintain them.

Why Boundaries Matter

1. **Personal Protection**
   Healthy boundaries keep you safe from harm or misuse. For instance, if a friend pressures you to do something that feels wrong, a clear boundary helps you stand your ground.
2. **Better Relationships**
   When you set boundaries, others know how to interact with you in ways that do not cause resentment or confusion. This clarity can make friendships and family ties calmer and more caring.
3. **Reduced Stress**
   If you do not set limits, you might take on too many tasks or accept negative behaviors from others. This can lead to exhaustion or emotional distress. Good boundaries prevent overload.
4. **Sense of Control**
   Boundaries remind you that you have a say in your own life. You are not a victim of circumstance; you can decide what is acceptable and what is not.

Common Types of Boundaries

1. **Physical Boundaries**
   This covers your personal space and body. Maybe you do not like people touching you without permission. Perhaps you prefer to keep a certain distance when talking. Clear physical boundaries allow you to feel comfortable in your environment.
2. **Emotional Boundaries**
   This is about how you share your feelings or personal information. You might choose not to discuss your private life with coworkers. Or you might set a limit on how much you listen to a friend vent about their problems without seeking help themselves.
3. **Mental Boundaries**
   This relates to your thoughts, beliefs, and ability to have your own opinions. If someone tries to force their viewpoint on you, a mental boundary involves expressing that you have a right to your perspective and prefer respectful discussion rather than arguments.
4. **Digital Boundaries**
   In today's world, digital space is part of life. Maybe you decide you will not answer work emails after 8:00 pm, or you choose not to share certain details on social media. This boundary protects your mental and emotional well-being in the digital realm.
5. **Material Boundaries**
   This involves how you share or protect your possessions. For example, you might have a rule that you do not lend out your car. Material boundaries prevent misunderstandings or potential misuse of your belongings.

How Boundaries Form in Childhood

Childhood experiences often shape how we handle boundaries. If your family did not allow you to say "no," you might have learned to put others' needs first. If your caregivers walked into your room without knocking, you might have grown up feeling you have no right to privacy. Conversely, if your parents respected your space and asked for your thoughts, you may have a healthier sense of when to say "yes" or "no" as an adult.

Key Childhood Factors:

- **Respect**: Did adults around you respect your property, space, or opinions?
- **Consent**: Were you allowed to refuse a hug or a visit if it made you uncomfortable?
- **Open Communication**: Could you speak openly about what made you feel uneasy without punishment?

If you grew up without these aspects, you might have trouble setting boundaries now. Recognizing this link can help you see why boundaries feel difficult or unnatural today.

Signs of Unhealthy Boundaries

1. **Feeling Overwhelmed**
   You say "yes" to things you do not want to do. You might feel burdened, resentful, or exhausted.
2. **Fear of Conflict**
   You let others cross your limits because you do not want an argument or fear being disliked.
3. **People-Pleasing**
   You ignore your own comfort to make others happy. This might cause stress, as you do things you truly dislike.
4. **Guilt After Saying "No"**
   Every time you say "no," you feel guilty or worried that you have done something wrong.
5. **Inability to Speak Your Mind**
   You do not share your thoughts, even when it is vital, because you fear confrontation or rejection.

Steps to Build Healthy Boundaries

Step 1: Identify Your Limits

Before you can set a boundary, you need to know what is acceptable to you. This might include:

- What kind of physical touch feels okay?
- How much personal information do you like to share?
- Which tasks or favors are you willing to do, and which ones are too much?

Write these down. Getting clear on your boundaries is the first step toward enforcing them.

Step 2: Understand Your Feelings

Tune in to any discomfort or irritation you feel in certain situations. That feeling can be a sign a boundary was crossed or is needed.

Step 3: Communicate Clearly

Setting a boundary often means telling people what you need. This might be as simple as, "I'd prefer if you call before coming over," or, "I need you to knock before entering my room." Short, direct statements are usually effective.

Step 4: Practice Saying "No"

Many struggle with "no" because they worry about hurting feelings. However, being truthful about your limits is kinder in the long run. Try a polite but firm approach: "Thanks for asking, but I can't help with that right now."

Step 5: Follow Through

A boundary that is stated but not enforced loses meaning. If someone repeatedly crosses a line, remind them of your stance. If they ignore it, consider steps to protect your well-being, such as spending less time with them if possible.

Handling Pushback

Some people will resist or argue when you set new boundaries—especially if they benefited from your lack of limits before. They might accuse you of being selfish or change how they treat you. This is not a sign that you are doing something wrong. It often means your boundary is working, and they are adjusting to a different dynamic.

- **Stay Calm**: Do not get pulled into a big argument. State your boundary again if needed.
- **Offer Understanding**: If they feel surprised, you can say, "I know this is different from how I used to act, but I need to respect my well-being now."
- **Be Prepared to Let Go**: If someone refuses to honor your boundary and continues to harm you, you might need to limit their access to your life.

Boundaries and the Inner Child

If your younger self did not learn that "no" is allowed, you might feel a pang of guilt or fear every time you try to set a boundary. Your inner child might worry about rejection or punishment. To heal this:

1. **Reassure Yourself**: Say quietly in your mind, "It's okay to say no. I won't be punished."
2. **Self-Soothing Tools**: If anxiety arises after setting a boundary, practice a quick calming trick, like taking a few slow breaths.
3. **Kind Inner Voice**: Remind yourself you matter and that your discomfort signals a need. Validate that need instead of dismissing it.

Over time, you teach your inner child that boundaries are normal and safe.

Practical Exercises for Strengthening Boundaries

Exercise 1: Boundary Mapping

1. Take a sheet of paper and draw three circles around a small figure labeled "Me."
2. Label the circles "Physical," "Emotional," and "Mental."
3. In each circle, write short notes: "Who can hug me without asking first?" "What topics do I keep private?" "When do I allow people to question my beliefs?"
4. Reflect on whether these circles match your current life. If they do not, note where you want to make changes.

Exercise 2: Daily Boundary Check

1. At the end of each day, think about any time you felt uneasy or stressed in interactions with others.
2. Ask yourself, "Which boundary might have been crossed?"
3. Write a short plan for how you can speak or act differently next time. Even if you do not change it yet, you raise your awareness.

Exercise 3: Role-Play with a Friend

1. Ask a friend or family member you trust to help you practice.
2. Give them a scenario, like borrowing your car without permission or pushing you to share personal details.
3. Practice stating your boundary: "I'm sorry, but I'm not comfortable with that."
4. Notice any hesitation or tension you feel. With practice, the words can flow more naturally.

Lesser-Known Tips for Managing Boundaries (Extra Useful Insights)

1. **Watch for Non-Verbal Cues**
   Sometimes, boundary crossing is not about words but actions or body language. If someone moves too close physically or stares at you in a way that feels uncomfortable, that is also a breach of your comfort zone. A firm, "Could you give me a bit more space, please?" can handle the situation without argument.
2. **Use "I" Statements**
   Instead of saying, "You are always too pushy," try, "I feel uneasy when I'm rushed. I'd like to move at my own pace." This keeps the focus on your need rather than blaming the other person.
3. **Know Your Exit Options**
   If you sense your boundary is not being respected, sometimes stepping away is best. This can mean leaving a social event early or ending a phone call. Having an exit plan reduces anxiety.
4. **Digital Boundaries Checklist**

    - Do you respond to texts late at night because you feel you have to?
    - Do you accept every friend request or read every email immediately?
    - Would limiting screen time help you relax more?
5. By reviewing these questions, you can see where you might set healthier digital boundaries.

Boundaries in Different Situations

Family

- **Respect for Privacy**: You might request that relatives do not show up at your home without calling first.
- **Holiday Events**: If you feel drained after long family gatherings, plan a time limit. Communicate it kindly: "I'll join for dinner but need to leave by 8:00 pm."

Workplace

- **Workload Limits**: If you cannot take on extra tasks, express that calmly and professionally.
- **Personal Topics**: If coworkers ask about sensitive issues, you can say, "I prefer not to discuss my personal life at work."

Friendships

- **Emotional Boundaries**: If a friend only talks about their problems and never listens to yours, let them know you need a more balanced exchange.
- **Shared Activities**: If you do not want to do a certain activity, say so. You do not have to force yourself to keep a friend happy if it conflicts with your comfort zone.

Romantic Relationships

- **Space and Time**: Let your partner know if you need personal time to recharge.
- **Topics You Are Not Ready to Discuss**: If you feel pressured to reveal something too soon, it is valid to say, "I'm not ready to share that yet."

- **Financial Boundaries**: Decide how you handle shared expenses and keep an open line of communication about money matters.

Handling Guilt and Anxiety When Setting Boundaries

It is normal to feel uneasy at first. Years of conditioning may have taught you to please everyone or avoid conflict. Here are ways to manage these feelings:

1. **Self-Reassurance**: Remind yourself that you are not hurting anyone by respecting your own needs.
2. **Prepare Simple Scripts**: Having a few rehearsed lines can reduce anxiety. For example, "I appreciate your request, but I can't do that now."
3. **Check the Facts**: Are you truly doing something harmful, or just doing something different from your past behavior? The difference matters.
4. **Seek Support**: Talk to friends or a counselor about the guilty feelings. They can remind you that self-care is not selfish.

Boundary Violations: What to Do

Sometimes, a person may keep crossing your boundaries, even after you have been clear. This can be draining and upsetting. Possible responses include:

- **A Second Reminder**: Restate your boundary: "I've asked you not to comment on my weight. Please respect that."
- **Consequences**: If they ignore you, you might choose not to spend time with them for a while, or you end the conversation immediately when they bring up the forbidden topic.
- **Seeking Mediation**: If the issue is with a family member or coworker, and it is severe, you might involve a neutral third party, like a therapist or HR professional, if appropriate.

Remember, a consistent follow-through shows you mean it.

How Boundaries Help Your Inner Child

Each time you set a boundary, you tell that younger side of yourself, "Your needs count." If your inner child felt unheard in the past, healthy boundaries can heal that wound. When you honor your limits, you become a trustworthy caretaker to yourself. This can reduce overall stress and help you grow a positive self-view.

Real-Life Examples of Healthy Boundaries

1. **Case: Janelle and Her Overly Critical Aunt**
   - **Situation**: Janelle's aunt frequently criticizes her lifestyle choices.
   - **Boundary**: Janelle tells her aunt, "I understand you have strong opinions, but I'd like it if we keep our conversations friendly. If you bring up my personal choices again, I'll step away from the conversation."
   - **Outcome**: Her aunt tries to push again, but Janelle leaves the chat. After a few times, the aunt scales back the criticism.
2. **Case: Tom and Late-Night Work Emails**
   - **Situation**: Tom's boss emails him late at night, expecting immediate responses.
   - **Boundary**: Tom politely writes, "I am off duty after 7 pm and will respond to any messages the next business day."
   - **Outcome**: At first, the boss protests, but Tom sticks to it. Over time, Tom notices less stress and better sleep, while still performing well at work.
3. **Case: Lucia and Her Friend's Frequent Emergencies**
   - **Situation**: Lucia's friend calls at all hours in crisis, expecting Lucia to fix every problem.
   - **Boundary**: Lucia explains that she cares but can only talk during reasonable hours. She also suggests the friend seek professional support.
   - **Outcome**: The friend gets upset at first, but Lucia feels relief at not being woken at 2 am. Over time, the friend learns to respect Lucia's limits or to reach out to a helpline instead.

Overcoming Obstacles to Setting Boundaries

1. **Fear of Being Labeled Selfish**: Remember that looking after your needs is not the same as ignoring others. You can still be kind and helpful within your limits.
2. **Self-Doubt**: You might question if your boundary is "right." There is no perfect rule, but if you feel your well-being is at stake, it is valid to set a limit.
3. **Past Trauma**: Negative experiences in childhood can cause panic or shame when you attempt to enforce boundaries. Seeking professional help can be a wise path if the anxiety is overwhelming.

Keeping Boundaries Flexible Yet Firm

Boundaries are not meant to be rigid walls that never shift. They can adapt based on your comfort level or changing life conditions. For instance, you might allow a close family member to drop by unannounced if you enjoy their presence, but not a casual acquaintance. Or you might need to adjust a rule at work during a busy season and then re-instate it later.

The key is to remain firm in your core principles—respect for your own well-being—while understanding that exceptions can be made if they genuinely suit your comfort level.

Lesser-Known Pitfalls and Tips to Avoid Them

1. **Over-Correcting**
   Sometimes, after years of no boundaries, a person might jump to extremely rigid boundaries that push everyone away. While self-protection is important, extreme isolation can backfire. Strike a balance.
2. **Passive Boundaries**
   Being vague about your limits—like subtly hinting or hoping others will notice your discomfort—often leads to confusion. Clear statements are kinder and more direct.

3. **Codependent Tendencies**
   If your identity is wrapped up in rescuing or pleasing others, setting boundaries might feel like losing your sense of self. In reality, it helps you form a healthier identity.
4. **Ignoring Your Body's Signals**
   Sometimes, your body reacts before you consciously realize a boundary is needed. Pay attention to a fast heartbeat, sudden tension, or a churning stomach. These might signal a line is being crossed.

Maintaining Progress

After you have set boundaries, it is crucial to check on them regularly:

- **Ask Yourself**: Are my boundaries still working for me?
- **Adjust If Needed**: If you find you have become too lenient or too strict, shift accordingly.
- **Acknowledge Growth**: Recognize the improvements in your life—maybe less stress or fewer conflicts. Let that confirm that boundaries are benefiting you.
- **Remain Open to Feedback**: If someone close to you feels hurt by a boundary, hear them out. You might clarify why the boundary matters or tweak it slightly if you feel comfortable.

Conclusion of Chapter 7

Healthy boundaries are vital for emotional wellness. They protect you from unnecessary stress and let you engage with others in a more balanced way. By taking the time to identify your limits, communicate them clearly, and enforce them with consistency, you show both yourself and your inner child that you deserve respect.

Yes, you may face pushback from those who liked things the old way, and you may wrestle with guilt or anxiety. But the long-term benefits—improved relationships, higher self-esteem, and a calmer mind—make it worthwhile. Remember that boundaries are a sign of self-respect, and they can help you move toward a healthier, more stable life.

CHAPTER 8: HANDLING SHAME AND GUILT

Introduction

Shame and guilt are strong feelings that can weigh on your heart and mind. Although they might seem similar, they are not the same. Guilt usually relates to what you have done, while shame relates to who you are. Both can become harmful if they take root and shape your self-view. Many people carry shame or guilt from early experiences, and these unresolved feelings can hold them back in adult life.

In this chapter, we will look at the differences between shame and guilt, explore how they might develop, and share methods for handling them. By learning to deal with these emotions, you can free yourself from the heavy cloud they create and allow your inner child to feel safer and more accepted.

Understanding Shame vs. Guilt

1. **Guilt**: "I did something wrong."
    - Guilt can be healthy if it leads to making amends or changing behavior. For instance, if you forget a friend's birthday, guilt might prompt you to apologize or make it up to them.
2. **Shame**: "There is something wrong with me."
    - Shame hits at the core of your identity. It can make you feel unworthy or flawed, even if you have not done anything obviously wrong. It can arise from hearing constant criticism as a child or from experiencing rejection or ridicule.

Roots of Shame and Guilt in Childhood

1. **Harsh Criticism**
   If adults around you used labels like "lazy," "bad," or "stupid," you might

have internalized these words. Over time, you can start to believe you are innately flawed.

2. **Strict Punishments**
   Constant scolding or harsh penalties for minor mistakes can cause a child to think, "I'm always in the wrong." This can turn into shame in later life.
3. **Cultural or Community Pressures**
   Some communities place heavy weight on certain behaviors or achievements. If you did not meet those expectations, you could carry guilt or shame for "letting them down."
4. **Unmet Emotional Needs**
   If you rarely received comfort, support, or praise, you might believe you are not deserving of kindness. This feeling often leads to shame.

The Harmful Effects of Ongoing Shame and Guilt

1. **Reduced Self-Worth**
   You might question your value, feeling you are not good enough in many areas of life.
2. **Self-Sabotage**
   Believing you are flawed can make you avoid opportunities. You might think, "I'm bound to fail anyway."
3. **Relationship Struggles**
   Shame can cause you to either cling to relationships out of fear of being alone or push people away because you assume they will reject you.
4. **Physical Stress**
   Long-term guilt or shame can strain your body, causing headaches, tension, or trouble sleeping.

Recognizing Unhealthy Shame and Guilt

Sometimes, guilt is appropriate if you truly harmed someone. But if you feel guilty for events you did not cause, or if you continue to punish yourself long after you have made things right, it becomes unhealthy. Similarly, shame is never healthy because it attacks your sense of self-worth.

Signs you are trapped in unhealthy shame or guilt:

- **Feeling worthless**: You think, "I am a bad person," as a constant mantra.
- **Taking blame for others' actions**: If a loved one is unhappy, you think it is all your fault.
- **Constant apology**: You say "sorry" all the time, even for minor or imagined faults.
- **Avoiding eye contact**: Shame can make you feel you do not deserve to be seen or heard.

Steps to Address Shame and Guilt

Step 1: Identify the Source

Ask yourself, "When did I first feel this way?" Try to recall the childhood events or repeated messages that led you to conclude you were at fault or unworthy.

Step 2: Separate Action from Identity

If guilt is linked to a specific action, focus on correcting that action or making amends. If the feeling persists even after that, you may have moved into shame territory—attacking yourself rather than the behavior.

Step 3: Challenge Negative Thoughts

Write down the negative things you say to yourself. Then ask, "Is this always true?" "Where is the proof?" Often, you will find these beliefs are based on old, hurtful messages rather than factual evidence.

Step 4: Make Amends Where Possible

If your guilt is connected to an actual wrongdoing, see if there is a way to fix it. This might involve apologizing, repaying a debt, or changing a habit that caused harm. Genuine action can ease real guilt.

Step 5: Offer Compassion to Yourself

Remember, everyone makes mistakes. Speak kindly to yourself as you would to a friend who is struggling. If you caught your friend in a spiral of shame, you would likely remind them of their good qualities. Practice that same care for yourself.

Handling the Emotional Weight of Guilt or Shame

Both guilt and shame can feel heavy in your body. You might notice tightness in your chest, a sinking feeling in your stomach, or an urge to isolate yourself. Below are ways to cope:

1. **Breathing Exercises**: Slow, deep breaths can calm the fight-or-flight response triggered by these emotions.
2. **Grounding Techniques**: Focus on the present moment by naming objects in the room, feeling the texture of your clothes, or identifying sounds around you. This helps you step out of the flood of negative thoughts.
3. **Mindful Acceptance**: Instead of pushing the feeling away, acknowledge it gently: "I feel shame right now. It's an emotion, not a fact about who I am."
4. **Movement**: Light physical movement can help release tension. A short walk or simple stretches might lessen the weight of the emotion.

Linking Shame and Guilt to the Inner Child

Often, the shame or guilt you feel as an adult originated from how you were treated as a child. If adults blamed you for their problems, you might still feel responsible for things beyond your control. Healing this link involves speaking to your inner child in a soothing way:

- **Validation**: "It wasn't your fault then, and it isn't your fault now."
- **Reassurance**: "You are not bad or broken. You deserve understanding."
- **Self-Parenting**: Give yourself the comfort or support you did not receive back then. This might be through journaling, affirmations, or therapy.

Real-Life Examples of Overcoming Shame and Guilt

1. **Case: Elijah and Academic Pressure**
    - **Situation**: Elijah grew up in a family that demanded top grades. When he did not excel in every subject, he was told he was "not trying."
    - **Adult Impact**: He felt shame about his intelligence, believing he was not smart enough.

    - **Approach**: Elijah wrote down actual facts: he graduated from college, succeeded in his career, and solved tough problems daily. He realized the family's standard was impossible. Over time, he replaced the shame message with, "I do my best, and that is enough."
2. **Case: Selena and Childhood Neglect**
    - **Situation**: Selena's caregiver was often absent, leaving her alone. She blamed herself, thinking, "I must not be lovable."
    - **Adult Impact**: She carried deep shame into her relationships, worried people would leave if they found out who she "really was."
    - **Approach**: Through counseling, she saw that her caregiver's absence was not her fault. She practiced repeating, "I am worthy of care," until it began to feel believable.
3. **Case: André and a Past Betrayal**
    - **Situation**: In his teens, André lied about a friend's secret, causing that friend to be hurt.
    - **Adult Impact**: He carried guilt for years, feeling he was a deceitful person.
    - **Approach**: André reached out and apologized sincerely, explaining he regretted his actions. Even if the friend did not fully forgive him, André did what he could to make amends. He learned to separate the harmful act he committed at 16 from his current adult self.

Practical Exercises to Release Shame and Guilt

Exercise 1: The "Write and Release" Method

1. Write a letter to the person or situation that caused you shame or guilt (you do not have to send it).
2. Describe how their words or actions affected you.
3. Tear up or safely burn the letter as a symbolic release.
4. Take a moment to breathe and note how you feel after letting it go physically.

Exercise 2: Self-Acceptance Script

1. Think of a recurring negative thought you have about yourself, such as "I am unworthy."
2. Write a simple script to counter it: "Even if I have made mistakes, I am still a person with good qualities. I deserve kindness."
3. Say this script out loud once a day for a week, paying attention to how it makes you feel.

Exercise 3: Healthy Affirmations Board

1. Create a small board or collage with kind words and images that represent self-worth and forgiveness.
2. Include statements like, "I grow from my mistakes," or "I deserve understanding."
3. Place the board somewhere visible, like near your desk or on your bedroom wall. Look at it when guilt or shame flares up.

The Value of Support in Dealing with Shame and Guilt

Trying to tackle shame and guilt alone can be tough. Sharing your burden with trusted people or professionals can ease the load:

- **Therapy**: A trained counselor can help you trace the roots of your shame or guilt and guide you toward healthier beliefs.
- **Support Groups**: Hearing from others with similar experiences can help you feel less isolated. You might learn new coping methods from them.
- **Close Friends or Family**: If you have supportive individuals in your life, let them know what you are feeling. They may offer a listening ear or comforting words.

Turning Guilt into Positive Change

Some guilt can be used constructively. If you know you hurt someone, genuine guilt can motivate you to apologize or behave better next time. The challenge is not to stay stuck in guilt once you have taken steps to address the harm. A few ideas:

1. **Learn the Lesson**: Ask, "What can I do differently to avoid repeating this?"
2. **Make a Plan**: If your guilt is about not spending enough time with family, plan a weekly call or visit.
3. **Forgive Yourself**: After you have done what you can to fix the situation, allow yourself to move on.

Healing Persistent Shame

Unlike guilt, shame often has no clear "fix" because it is tied to your sense of self. You can, however, begin to heal it:

1. **Write Positive Traits**: List qualities you like about yourself, even if it feels awkward.
2. **Engage in Activities You Enjoy**: Success in small things—like learning a new recipe or finishing a book—can remind you that you are capable and valuable.
3. **Practice Self-Kindness Daily**: Each time you catch a shame thought, gently replace it with a statement of self-acceptance. This is a long process, but repetition can slowly reshape your self-image.

How This Links to Boundaries

Shame and guilt can weaken your ability to set boundaries. If you feel unworthy, you might let people walk all over you or fail to express your needs. By working on shame and guilt, you strengthen your sense of self, making it easier to say "no" or speak up. Conversely, good boundaries can reduce shame and guilt by ensuring others treat you with respect.

Lesser-Known Ways to Ease Shame and Guilt

1. **Sharing Through Art**
   Painting, drawing, or sculpting how shame or guilt feels can help you

externalize the emotion. Seeing it as a separate creation might make it feel less overwhelming.

2. **Identify "Inherited" Shame**
   Sometimes, you carry shame passed down from relatives who were shamed themselves (for instance, due to poverty, mental health issues, or family secrets). Recognizing that you are carrying someone else's burden can help you release it.
3. **Posture Check**
   Notice how your body reacts when you feel shame. Do your shoulders slump? Do you look down? Try standing up straight, lifting your head, and taking a deep breath. Adjusting your posture can shift your mental state.
4. **Quiet Self-Hate With Facts**
   If you find yourself thinking, "I can't do anything right," write down at least three tasks you did well in the past week. Countering negative self-talk with real examples is more powerful than you might think.

Handling Relapses

Feelings of shame or guilt might return even after you have made progress. This is normal. An old trigger—a harsh comment, a memory—can bring them back. Instead of feeling defeated:

- **Recognize the Trigger**: Identify what caused the return of shame or guilt.
- **Use Your Tools**: Whether it is a breathing exercise, journaling, or calling a friend, bring out the methods that helped before.
- **Remind Yourself of Growth**: Think of how you handled this emotion in the past and how you are coping better now.

How Healing Shame and Guilt Affects the Inner Child

When you address these painful emotions, you free the younger part of you from blame. That child might have spent years feeling there was something wrong with them. By learning that you are deserving of respect and kindness, you send a powerful signal of reassurance to your inner child. This can bring a lighter, more hopeful view of yourself and your life possibilities.

Conclusion of Chapter 8

Shame and guilt, though common, can be deeply harmful if left unaddressed. Guilt, in a healthy form, guides you to correct mistakes. Shame, however, questions your value as a person and can cause long-term damage to how you see yourself. Understanding where these emotions come from and applying specific strategies—such as challenging negative beliefs, making amends, and practicing self-compassion—can lighten their grip on you.

As you grow in this area, you will likely find it easier to set boundaries, try new things without fearing constant failure, and connect with others in a more open way. Most importantly, you show your inner child that they do not deserve condemnation for past events outside their control. In the next chapters, we will move into more topics related to personal relationships and building support systems, which often require a healthier relationship with yourself free from toxic shame or guilt.

CHAPTER 9: RELATIONSHIPS AND SUPPORT SYSTEMS

Introduction

People are social beings. From early childhood, we learn to rely on family, friends, and other key individuals for emotional care and practical help. As you grow older, these connections can expand and change, but the basic need for reliable relationships remains. For someone who is healing their inner child, trusting others might feel risky. Past experiences of hurt or neglect can leave you cautious or unsure about seeking support.

In this chapter, we will look at why relationships and support systems matter, how to build and maintain them in healthy ways, and what to watch out for in potentially harmful connections. By the end, you will have guidelines for identifying safe people, communicating your needs, and balancing self-care with group ties. These steps are important for creating a life where you feel valued and less alone.

The Value of Connection

1. **Emotional Warmth**
   Healthy relationships offer understanding, comfort, and a sense of belonging. When you share positive moments or hardships with supportive individuals, you are reminded that you do not have to handle life alone.
2. **Practical Help**
   Sometimes you need practical support—like someone who can watch your pet while you are away or give you feedback on a tough situation. Close ties can make these tasks easier.
3. **Personal Growth**
   Spending time with people who care about you can help you develop better communication, empathy, and conflict-resolution skills. You learn by observing and practicing healthy behaviors in a safe setting.

4. **Inner Child Reassurance**
   Positive connections can send your inner child a new message: "There are people who listen to and respect you." This helps replace old ideas of being unheard or uncared for.

Different Types of Relationships

- **Family**: This can include relatives by blood, marriage, or adoption. Family ties can be deeply nurturing or very complicated.
- **Friendships**: These connections can range from casual acquaintances to best friends you trust completely.
- **Romantic**: These are intimate partnerships, often involving emotional and possibly physical closeness.
- **Professional**: The relationships you have at work or school, which can still provide mutual support and understanding.
- **Online Communities**: In the digital age, some people find safe spaces on the internet where they can share problems, hobbies, or personal stories.

Each type has its own boundaries, expectations, and potential benefits. Sometimes, a problem in one type of relationship can spill into others, which is why building healthy connection skills is valuable in all areas of life.

Building Safe and Supportive Bonds

1. Know What You Need
Before forming new bonds or deepening existing ones, it helps to be clear about what you want. Are you seeking someone to talk to about personal feelings, or do you just want a casual friend to share hobbies with? Being honest with yourself can guide you toward the right people.

2. Start Slowly
Friendships and close connections usually develop over time. Share a little about yourself, see how the other person responds, and allow the bond to deepen step by step. This slower pace helps you see if the relationship is trustworthy.

3. Choose Individuals Who Show Respect
Look for people who listen without attacking, judge less, and treat you with understanding. If you notice someone often looks down on others or mocks them, consider whether they will truly respect your needs.

4. Check for Give-and-Take
Healthy connections usually involve both giving and receiving. You offer support or kindness, and the other person does the same. If you find yourself always giving, or if the other person is always taking, the relationship might feel draining.

5. Communicate Your Comfort Zones
If you have certain limits—like specific topics you do not want to discuss—make them clear. A respectful friend or partner will understand and not push you in uncomfortable ways.

Communication Basics in Building Good Relationships

1. Active Listening

- Look at the person speaking (if you are in the same place).
- Ask short questions if you do not understand.
- Summarize what you heard to confirm you got it right.

2. Clear Expression of Your Feelings

- Use simple "I" statements like, "I feel upset when I'm ignored," instead of "You always ignore me."
- Describe the specific behavior that bothers you and why.

3. Honesty Over Perfection

- You do not have to say everything in the most eloquent way. It is more important to be sincere. If you fumble your words, clarify what you meant and keep going.

4. Balancing Talking and Listening

- Let others share as well. If you are always the one talking, or always the one listening, the connection can become unbalanced.

Red Flags in Friendships or Partnerships

Unfortunately, not all relationships are safe or supportive. Here are signs that a connection might be unhealthy:

1. **Criticism of Your Core Self**: If the person constantly insults who you are—your looks, your intelligence, or your personal traits—it can harm your self-esteem.
2. **Control Tactics**: If they try to manage your time, your friendships, or your decisions, watch out. Healthy relationships allow personal freedom.
3. **Gaslighting**: This is when someone makes you doubt your own memory or perception. They might say, "That never happened," even though you recall it clearly. This behavior confuses you and undermines your sense of reality.
4. **Excessive Jealousy**: Feeling a little jealous now and then is normal, but if someone is always suspicious or making accusations, it can become toxic.
5. **Unequal Effort**: If you notice you are doing all the work to keep the connection alive—always calling, always arranging meetings—without any effort from them, it might not be a healthy bond.

Dealing with Conflict

Conflict happens in every human bond. It is not the conflict itself that matters, but how you handle it.

1. **Stay Calm**: Take a moment to breathe if you feel anger rising.
2. **Focus on the Issue**: Try not to bring up past unrelated matters. Tackle one issue at a time.
3. **Avoid Name-Calling**: Personal attacks can damage trust.
4. **Seek Solutions**: Ask, "How can we fix this?" instead of dwelling on blame.
5. **Agree to Disagree**: Sometimes, you will not reach a perfect consensus. It is okay to respect each other's viewpoints without forcing a complete match.

When done respectfully, conflict can bring deeper understanding. Both parties might learn each other's boundaries and preferences better.

Support Systems Through Different Life Stages

Your needs for support might change as you go through life. For instance:

- **Teens and Early Adults**: You might rely heavily on friends and mentors for guidance about school, career, and identity.
- **New Parents**: Building connections with other parents can be crucial, as they understand the challenges of raising kids.
- **Mid-Life Changes**: Work pressures, health concerns, or caring for aging relatives might lead you to look for more varied support, including professionals or community programs.
- **Later Years**: Loneliness can become a concern, so staying linked to neighbors, groups, or social clubs may help maintain a sense of belonging.

It is normal for your social circle to shift over time. The key is to remain open to forming new bonds and adjusting old ones based on your current circumstances.

The Inner Child's Need for Support

When you recognize that your younger self was possibly ignored or dismissed, it might feel very risky to open up to others now. However, supportive ties can offer the acceptance and understanding the inner child never received.

- **Practice Sharing Small Vulnerabilities**: Start by telling a friend or group something minor that feels a bit personal. Observe how they respond. If you feel safe, you can gradually share a bit more.
- **Explain Your Boundaries**: If you are not ready to talk about certain childhood events, say so. A good friend will not pressure you.
- **Look for Honest Encouragement**: Notice if people cheer you on in a genuine way, not to manipulate or to get something from you.

Over time, your inner child can learn that there are trustworthy individuals who do care. This lessens the burden of old pain.

Overcoming Isolation

Some people isolate themselves due to past hurts, fear of rejection, or low trust in others. While short breaks from social contact can be healthy, long-term isolation can worsen feelings of loneliness or self-doubt. Here are steps to break out of that pattern:

1. **Start Small**: Attend a local meet-up or a hobby group once a month. Gradually increase social activities.
2. **Online Communities**: If in-person contact is too stressful, start by joining a supportive online group. Interact at a pace that feels comfortable.
3. **Personal Projects**: Invite a friend or neighbor to join a creative project, such as painting a room or planting a small garden. Shared activities can strengthen bonds without intense emotional exposure.
4. **Professional Help**: If your isolation stems from deeper trauma, consider seeking a counselor for guidance and support.

Real-Life Examples of Building Good Support Systems

1. **Case: Mia's Move to a New City**
   - **Situation**: Mia felt lonely after relocating for work. She had no close friends in the new place.
   - **Action**: She joined a weekend hiking club and started chatting with fellow hikers. Over time, she found two people she connected with. They began meeting outside the club for coffee.
   - **Outcome**: Mia built a small network of supportive individuals who helped her adjust to her new environment.
2. **Case: Ravi's Family Struggles**
   - **Situation**: Ravi's parents had always been distant, and he felt lonely in family gatherings.
   - **Action**: He reached out to an uncle who seemed understanding. They met monthly for dinner, talking about common interests and emotional topics.
   - **Outcome**: While his relationship with his parents remained strained, Ravi found comfort in another family member. This helped him feel less isolated.
3. **Case: Anya's Trust Issues**

- **Situation**: Anya had been betrayed by close friends in her teenage years. She avoided forming deep ties for fear of being hurt again.
- **Action**: She started attending group therapy sessions once a week. Hearing others' stories encouraged her to share a bit of her own. The non-judgmental response she got boosted her trust in human connection.
- **Outcome**: Anya formed a new friend from the group who respected her limits. This slowly restored her ability to open up.

Practical Exercises for Strengthening Relationships and Support

Exercise 1: Communication Goals

1. Pick one person in your life you want to connect with better.
2. Write down a short-term goal, such as, "I want to have a calm chat about a sensitive issue."
3. Plan how you will start the conversation. For example, "Hey, I'd like to talk about something that's been on my mind. Is now a good time?"
4. Afterward, note what went well and what you might do differently next time.

Exercise 2: Support Map

1. Draw a circle in the center of a paper labeled "Me."
2. Around it, write the names of people or groups you trust or could turn to in different areas (emotional support, practical help, etc.).
3. If you notice blank areas—like no one to go to for advice on finances—think about where you might find that support (a financial counselor, a colleague good with money, etc.).

Exercise 3: Practicing Boundaries in Conversation

1. Notice a situation where you tend to overshare or stay silent out of fear.
2. Plan a response that keeps you comfortable. For instance, if a coworker asks about a personal topic you do not want to discuss, your prepared

line might be, "I'm not ready to talk about that, but how about we chat about something else?"
3. Use this phrase or a similar one the next time it happens. Notice how you feel afterward.

Lesser-Known Tips for Healthy Connection (Extra Useful Insights)

1. **Ask for Clarity**
   Instead of guessing what someone means, calmly ask, "Could you tell me more about that?" This prevents misunderstandings and shows genuine interest in the other person's thoughts.
2. **Offer Help Wisely**
   Helping others can build warm connections, but be aware of your limits. If you overextend yourself, you might become resentful or exhausted. Check if you have the time and energy before saying yes.
3. **Set Interaction Windows**
   If texting or social media chat drains you, consider telling friends, "I'm not always online. I'll reply when I can." This is a healthy digital boundary that lowers pressure.
4. **Stay Curious**
   Ask open-ended questions about someone's life, hobbies, or viewpoints. People often appreciate genuine interest, and this can spark deeper conversations.

Maintaining Relationships Over Time

Building a bond is one thing, but keeping it going as life changes is another.

- **Regular Check-Ins**: Send a short text or make a quick call to say hello if you have not chatted in a while.
- **Update Each Other**: Share changes in your life, both the good and the tough. This helps friends or family know what you are going through.
- **Be Willing to Adapt**: If a friend has less time due to a new job or baby, adjust how you interact. Maybe shorter calls or quick coffee meets instead of lengthy hangouts.

- **Resolve Tension Early**: If an issue arises, address it calmly rather than letting resentment grow.

Over time, mutual respect, understanding, and flexible responses to life's changes keep relationships strong and beneficial.

What If Support Isn't Available Nearby?

Some people find themselves in a place with few trusted individuals or limited opportunities to meet others. In that case:

1. **Online Groups**: Join safe, moderated communities that focus on your interests or needs (mental health forums, hobby clubs, educational groups).
2. **Classes or Workshops**: Look for virtual or local classes that teach a skill you are curious about. The shared interest can help spark friendships.
3. **Seek Professional Support**: Therapists, counselors, or helplines can fill a gap when personal relationships are lacking. Over time, they can also guide you toward building a more personal network.

Balancing Self-Reliance with Shared Support

Yes, it is important to learn self-care skills and develop inner strength. But leaning on others does not mean you are weak. It is okay to handle some issues alone and seek help for others. This balance of self-reliance and connection is healthy:

- **When to Seek Help**: If you are facing a challenge you have never handled before, or if you feel emotionally overwhelmed, reaching out can prevent bigger crises.
- **When to Rely on Yourself**: For routine or daily tasks you know how to manage, you can keep your independence.

Over time, you will get a feel for when to turn to others and when to solve things on your own.

How Strong Support Helps the Inner Child

When your adult self has caring and reliable bonds, the part of you that once felt alone or unseen can gradually relax. Each positive interaction says, "You are not alone anymore." This comfort can speed up the healing of emotional wounds and make new growth possible.

Conclusion of Chapter 9

Relationships and support systems are crucial for emotional well-being. They give you comfort, lessons, and help you cannot always provide for yourself. Yet these connections can also stir up fear or caution, especially if your inner child experienced betrayal or neglect. By learning to spot healthy connections, communicate your needs, and handle conflict wisely, you build a network that supports you at every stage of life.

Remember, it is okay to begin small and gradually let others in. A friendly coworker, a community group, or an online peer can be the start of a new sense of safety. Overcoming past hurts takes time, but with consistent practice of clear communication and balanced sharing, you create strong bonds that remind you that you matter.

In the next chapter, we will focus on overcoming fear—another major roadblock for many who are trying to heal their inner child. Fear can prevent you from forming the relationships we discussed in this chapter, so learning to handle it is another key step in your overall healing process.

CHAPTER 10: OVERCOMING FEAR

Introduction

Fear is a normal response when you sense potential harm or danger. Without some fear, you might take reckless actions. However, excessive or persistent fear can hold you back from living a full life. It might stop you from meeting new people, trying new things, or stepping outside old patterns. If your inner child has memories of scary events or emotional harm, fear can become a constant background feeling, affecting how you view the world.

This chapter explores what fear is, where it comes from, how it affects the body and mind, and practical methods to reduce its negative effects. You will learn to identify healthy caution versus unhelpful worry, and how to move forward even when you are nervous. Overcoming fear—or at least reducing it to a manageable level—can open doors to better relationships, personal growth, and a sense of freedom.

The Nature of Fear

Fear is a protective emotion. In a dangerous situation, your heart races, your muscles tense, and your mind focuses on survival. This reaction can help you run faster or fight if necessary. In today's world, though, many fears are not about immediate physical threats. They might be about rejection, failure, or the unknown.

When fear shows up too often or at the wrong times, it can cause problems:

- You might avoid opportunities out of worry you will mess up.
- You might stay silent in group settings, fearing judgment.
- You might feel panicked in harmless situations, such as meeting new people or traveling to unfamiliar places.

Understanding fear's purpose can help you see it is not the enemy; rather, it is a signal. The next step is deciding which signals are worth acting on and which are not.

Types of Fear

1. **Fear of Failure**
   You worry that if you try something and it does not work out, others will judge you or you will feel shame.
2. **Fear of Abandonment**
   Stemming from childhood neglect or loss, this fear can cause you to cling to relationships or avoid them altogether so you will not be hurt.
3. **Fear of Being Judged**
   You might constantly think others are watching and criticizing you, which can lead to self-consciousness in social settings.
4. **Fear of the Unknown**
   When stepping into a new job, a new city, or any unfamiliar territory, you might feel anxious because you do not know what to expect.
5. **Phobias**
   These are intense fears about specific things or situations—like heights, animals, or enclosed spaces. They often go beyond simple caution and can trigger panic.

Impact of Fear on the Mind and Body

- **Physical Symptoms**: Sweating, rapid heartbeat, shaking, and stomach discomfort can all appear when fear strikes.
- **Mental Fog**: It can be hard to think clearly or make decisions. Your mind might race or shut down under intense fear.
- **Sleep Problems**: Frequent fear or worry can keep you awake at night, leading to insomnia.
- **Social Withdrawal**: Over time, avoiding what you fear can shrink your world. You skip events, do not apply for better jobs, or stay away from new experiences.

Common Childhood Origins of Fear

1. **Traumatic Events**
   This can include physical harm, bullying, or witnessing violence. A child

who grows up in a threatening environment may carry that sense of threat into adulthood.

2. **Repeated Warnings**
   If caregivers were overly protective or anxious, you might have learned that the world is full of dangers. This can shape your own fears as you grow.
3. **Shame or Criticism**
   If every mistake was harshly punished, you might now fear trying new things in case you fail.
4. **Sudden Loss or Separation**
   If someone close to you disappeared from your life unexpectedly, you could develop fear of abandonment that affects your current relationships.

The Connection Between Fear and the Inner Child

When your inner child is afraid, it may show up as adult behaviors you cannot fully explain, such as:

- **Overreacting to Minor Risks**: Feeling panic over small challenges because they remind you of bigger threats from childhood.
- **Freezing Up**: Being unable to speak or act when fear spikes.
- **Seeking Constant Reassurance**: You might need others to confirm you are safe or okay, reflecting the lack of security you felt as a child.

By identifying these reactions as echoes of past experiences, you can begin to reassure your inner child that you have more resources and power now. You are no longer trapped in the old situation.

Coping Tools for Fear

1. **Grounding Exercises**
   - Focus on the present moment by naming five things you see around you, four things you can touch, three things you can hear, two you can smell, and one you can taste.

    - This method pulls your mind away from fear and onto concrete reality.
2. **Breathing Techniques**
    - Try a slow count: Breathe in for four, hold for two, breathe out for four. Repeat until you feel calmer.
    - Deep breathing lowers tension and sends a signal to your body that the threat level is decreasing.
3. **Muscle Relaxation**
    - Tense and release muscle groups from your feet up to your head. This helps reduce the physical grip of fear.
4. **Positive Self-Talk**
    - Use phrases like, "I can handle this," or "I am safe right now." This counters the messages of panic.
5. **Safe Visualization**
    - Picture a place or memory where you felt secure, such as a quiet park or a cozy corner. Spend a minute with that image to calm your nervous system.

Practical Strategies to Overcome Fear

Strategy 1: Gradual Exposure

If possible, face your fear in small steps rather than all at once. For example, if you fear social events, start by attending a small gathering and leaving after 30 minutes, or meet with just one new person. Over time, you can handle larger social settings.

Strategy 2: Fact-Checking

Ask yourself, "What am I really afraid of here?" and "How likely is it to happen?" Often, fear grows because we imagine worst-case scenarios without examining the odds. By checking facts, you might see the danger is smaller than you first thought.

Strategy 3: Plan B or Plan C

Sometimes having a backup plan can ease fear. If you worry about getting stuck in a new place, plan how you will exit or whom you can call if something goes wrong. This sense of preparation lowers anxiety.

Strategy 4: Celebrate Small Wins

Each time you do something that used to frighten you—even a tiny step—acknowledge it. Make a simple note in a journal: "I spoke up in a meeting today." Recognizing progress helps your mind believe you can overcome fear.

Strategy 5: Seek Professional Support

If fear is very strong or connected to serious trauma, a trained counselor can guide you. They can introduce more advanced techniques, such as systematic desensitization or cognitive restructuring, in a secure environment.

Real-Life Examples of Overcoming Fear

1. **Case: Carlos's Fear of Public Speaking**
    - **Situation**: Carlos froze whenever he had to speak in front of a group, even if it was just five people.
    - **Roots**: In childhood, a teacher mocked him for stuttering during a presentation.
    - **Approach**: Carlos joined a small public speaking group that practiced short presentations. He started with a 1-minute talk, then built up to 5 minutes.
    - **Outcome**: Gradually, his fear eased. He still felt nerves, but they did not stop him from speaking.
2. **Case: Marian's Fear of Rejection**
    - **Situation**: Marian avoided dating and making new friends. She believed people would eventually reject her if they discovered her flaws.
    - **Roots**: She had a distant parent who often left home for weeks with no explanation. As a child, she felt it was her fault.
    - **Approach**: Marian worked with a counselor to understand that her parent's actions were not caused by her. She practiced meeting people for short coffee chats instead of longer outings, reducing the anxiety around rejection.
    - **Outcome**: Marian made a supportive friend who respected her slower pace. Over time, she grew more comfortable letting people into her life.
3. **Case: Luke's Fear of Swimming**

- **Situation**: Luke had almost drowned as a child and became terrified of all bodies of water.
- **Approach**: He took lessons with an instructor specialized in fear-based issues. They started with gentle water contact, like standing on the pool steps, then submerging just his feet.
- **Outcome**: After several weeks, Luke managed to swim short distances with a float. While the fear did not vanish completely, he felt safe enough to enjoy being in the water with caution.

Lesser-Known Methods for Handling Fear (Extra Useful Insights)

1. **Labeling Emotions**
   - Sometimes, you feel anxious but do not realize it is fear. Labeling the feeling clearly—"I'm feeling scared"—can help you face it directly instead of avoiding it.
2. **Ask: "What Would I Tell a Friend?"**
   - If a friend had the same fear, how would you reassure them or help them see options? Apply that advice to yourself.
3. **Use Humor**
   - If possible, gently laugh at the exaggerated worries your mind creates. You might say, "I'm acting like stepping on stage means I'm battling a dragon." Humor can reduce fear's intensity.
4. **Check Your Body Signals**
   - Notice if your shoulders are tense or your jaw is clenched. Sometimes, relaxing these areas helps lower fear.
5. **Physical Activities**
   - Exercise, dance, or even simple stretches release tension and produce hormones that balance your mood.

Dealing with Setbacks in Managing Fear

Even with good strategies, you may face moments when fear overwhelms you again. That does not mean you have failed. It simply indicates that fear is persistent and needs ongoing attention.

- **Stay Patient**: Progress is not always a straight path.

- **Review Your Tools**: Return to grounding, breathing, or small-step methods.
- **Talk About It**: Share the setback with a trusted friend or counselor. They can remind you how far you have come and help you refocus.
- **Celebrate Even Minor Gains**: If you managed to reduce a panic attack from 20 minutes to 10 minutes, that is still progress.

Moving Past Fear Without Shame

Sometimes, people feel embarrassed about their fears, especially if they seem "small" to others. However, each person's emotional triggers are unique. Shaming yourself for being afraid only adds an extra layer of negativity.

- **Self-Acceptance**: Recognize that the fear is there for a reason, often linked to past events or learned behaviors.
- **Educate Yourself**: Read about how fear works in the brain. It helps to see that fear is a universal human response.
- **Speak Kindly to Yourself**: Use a gentle tone in your thoughts. "It's okay to be afraid. I'm working on it."

How Overcoming Fear Helps the Inner Child

When you face your fears in a careful, supportive way, you show your inner child that times have changed. The frightening experiences from the past do not have to rule your present life. Each step you take to reduce fear offers comfort and assurance to the younger you who once felt helpless.

Practical Exercises for Managing Fear

Exercise 1: Fear Ladder

1. Write down one fear—for example, talking to strangers.
2. List small actions from easiest to hardest: (1) saying "hello" to one stranger in a shop, (2) asking a simple question (like directions), (3) having a short chat, (4) joining a social event with people you do not know.

3. Start at the easiest step, repeat it until you are more comfortable, then move to the next.

Exercise 2: Worst-Case, Best-Case, Most Likely

1. Think about a current worry—maybe a job interview or a tough conversation.
2. Write the worst-case scenario: "I freeze and cannot speak, and they think I'm totally incompetent."
3. Write the best-case scenario: "I speak confidently, they love my ideas, and I get exactly what I hoped for."
4. Write the most likely scenario: "I will be a bit nervous, but I'll answer the questions okay. It might be a little awkward, but it's not a disaster."
5. Notice how focusing on the realistic middle ground helps reduce extreme fear.

Exercise 3: Daily Calm Time

1. Carve out five or ten minutes each day to sit quietly.
2. Observe your thoughts, letting them come and go without fighting them. If fear thoughts arise, label them as "just thoughts."
3. Practice slow breathing or simple stretching to help your body relax.
4. Over time, this routine can train your mind and body to calm down more quickly when fear strikes in other situations.

Next Steps for Long-Term Change

Overcoming strong or chronic fear often requires consistent practice and patience. It is not about eliminating fear entirely, but about learning to live without letting fear run your decisions.

- **Keep Tracking Your Progress**: Note improvements or times you acted despite being scared.
- **Adjust Techniques**: If one method does not help, try another. Each person's fear pattern is unique, so you might need a tailored approach.

- **Consider Counseling or Group Support**: Especially if fear is tied to past trauma. A trained professional can guide you more deeply into methods like exposure therapy or cognitive restructuring.
- **Pair Up**: Find a friend or buddy who also wants to tackle a fear. You can encourage each other, share tips, and hold each other accountable.

Conclusion of Chapter 10

Fear can be both a friend and a challenge. It warns you of real dangers, but it can also grow too large when shaped by childhood experiences or negative self-beliefs. By understanding the roots of fear, using tools like grounding and slow exposure, and seeking support when needed, you can move forward with greater confidence. This does not mean you never feel afraid—it means fear no longer dictates your path.

As your inner child witnesses these steps, they gradually learn that the old dangers do not control your life now. The adult you is capable of providing safety and making reasoned decisions. This greater sense of security is a crucial part of healing. In the chapters ahead, you will continue building self-worth and exploring practical methods to sustain the gains you have made so far.

CHAPTER 11: SELF-WORTH

Introduction

Self-worth is the sense that you have value simply by existing. It is not something you must earn through accomplishments, money, or praise. Rather, it is an inner understanding that you, as a person, deserve respect and kindness. Many people confuse self-worth with self-esteem, but they are slightly different. Self-esteem is often tied to what you do—like how you feel about your work or your abilities. Self-worth runs deeper. It is about knowing you have value even if you fail, make mistakes, or struggle.

In childhood, you might not have received messages that built this sense of worth. Some children are criticized or ignored by adults who themselves lacked self-worth. Others find they get approval only when they perform well in school or meet certain standards. These early experiences can leave you doubting your value as an adult. This chapter will explain how self-worth forms, why it might be weakened, and what you can do to rebuild it.

The Roots of Self-Worth

Self-worth typically begins forming in your earliest years. Caregivers who show love without conditions—offering warmth and support whether you excel or stumble—tend to raise children who feel worthy inside. In contrast, if you grew up having to earn acceptance or if you faced constant disapproval, you might have learned that love and respect are conditional. This can lead to an unstable sense of value in adult life.

Key childhood factors that shape self-worth include:

1. **Unconditional Support**
   When an adult shows that they love and respect you even when you fail at a task, you learn you are acceptable as a person, not just as a performer.
2. **Consistent Warmth**
   If caregivers are usually cold or distracted, you might sense that you are not important. This message can grow into a belief that you are unworthy of care.

3. **Reasonable Boundaries**
   Boundaries that are fair show a child that their needs matter but that they also live in a shared environment. If boundaries are harsh or always changing, the child can feel insecure about who they are and what they deserve.
4. **Verbal and Non-Verbal Cues**
   The words, tone, and body language of caregivers shape how you see yourself. Sarcasm, put-downs, or ignoring can signal that you do not matter. In contrast, gentle words, smiles, and real listening convey that you are worthy of attention.

These early patterns can follow you into adulthood, influencing how you see yourself and whether you believe you deserve positive things.

Signs of Low Self-Worth

1. **Negative Self-Talk**
   Constantly calling yourself "stupid," "lazy," or "no good" in your mind is a clue that you do not see your true value.
2. **People-Pleasing**
   You might do things you dislike or push yourself beyond your limits to get others' approval, because you do not think you have worth otherwise.
3. **Fear of Failure**
   If you see mistakes as evidence that you are worthless, you might avoid taking any risks or trying new things.
4. **Struggling to Accept Praise**
   When others compliment you, you might dismiss it or think they are not sincere, because you do not believe good things about yourself.
5. **Inability to Set Boundaries**
   Without a sense of inherent worth, you might let others walk all over you or ignore your feelings to avoid conflict.

Why Self-Worth Matters

1. **Mental Well-Being**
   A stable sense of self-worth helps you handle stress and challenges without feeling crushed. It lays a foundation for mental balance.

2. **Healthy Relationships**
   People with a basic sense of value are less likely to depend on others for constant validation. This makes for more balanced interactions.
3. **Resilience**
   When you know you have worth, you can face failures or setbacks with less emotional turmoil. You can learn from mistakes instead of feeling defined by them.
4. **Personal Growth**
   Believing you have value encourages you to try new skills or tasks. You do not see challenges as threats to your identity but as steps in learning.

How to Build Self-Worth

1. Recognize Inaccurate Beliefs

Ask yourself: "Where did I get the idea that I am not worthy?" Often, you might find it was from a person or event in your childhood that does not reflect the full truth about you.

2. Practice Self-Affirmation

Create statements that are kind and basic, such as, "I matter even when I struggle," or "My existence has value regardless of my achievements." Repeat them daily, even if it feels awkward at first.

3. Challenge Negative Thoughts

When you catch yourself thinking, "I am worthless," write it down. Then ask, "Is there proof of this?" More often than not, you will find that it is simply an old, damaging thought, not a fact.

4. Treat Yourself with Respect

Ask: "If I truly believed I was worthy, how would I act today?" Perhaps you would say no to an extra request at work or speak up if a friend is unkind. Start practicing these behaviors.

5. Find a Supportive Environment

Seek out people who show kindness and acknowledge your worth. If you stay around those who belittle you, it is harder to form a stable sense of value.

Common Barriers to Building Self-Worth

1. **Perfectionism**
   If you think you must do everything flawlessly to be valuable, you set yourself up for constant self-criticism.
2. **Past Trauma**
   Serious emotional or physical harm in childhood can ingrain a deep sense of being "less than." Professional help may be crucial here.
3. **Comparisons**
   Always measuring yourself against others can erode your sense of worth. There will always be someone with different talents or advantages.
4. **Doubting Compliments**
   You might reject positive feedback with thoughts like, "They are just being nice," blocking it from boosting your self-worth.

Helping the Inner Child See Their Worth

For many adults with low self-worth, the child inside is carrying beliefs from a time when they were powerless. To help that younger side of yourself:

- **Visualize Giving Comfort**: Picture yourself talking to the child you once were. Offer words of kindness and reassurance.
- **Rewrite the Old Story**: If you were told, "You will never be good enough," imagine telling your younger self, "They were wrong. You have value, and I see it now."
- **Create Small Rituals**: Perhaps you set aside a moment each day to do something small but comforting—like writing a one-line note of encouragement or hugging a soft pillow. This shows your inner child you are willing to provide care now.

Practical Exercises to Strengthen Self-Worth

Exercise 1: Daily Worth Reminder

1. Get a small notebook or note-taking app.

2. Each day, write one thing that you value about yourself. It can be as simple as, "I said a kind word to someone," or "I made a decent attempt at cooking."
3. Do this for at least two weeks. At the end, read through your list. This practice trains your mind to notice positive things about you.

Exercise 2: Self-Worth Collage

1. Gather magazines, pictures, or words that represent things you appreciate about yourself.
2. Glue or tape them onto a piece of paper or board.
3. Place it somewhere visible—like above your desk or near your bed. Remind yourself that these qualities exist, even if you have a tough day.

Exercise 3: The "I Am" Statement

1. Write down 5–10 statements starting with "I am..." (Examples: "I am caring," "I am creative," "I am helpful.")
2. Do not dismiss them as small. Review these statements regularly—especially when self-doubt creeps in.
3. If you struggle to find statements, think about how friends or kind acquaintances might describe you.

Negative Influences on Self-Worth and How to Address Them

1. **Toxic Relationships**
    - If someone in your life belittles you, it might reinforce the idea that you lack worth.
    - **Solution**: Limit time with such people if possible, or set firm boundaries. Remind yourself that you do not have to accept hurtful words.
2. **Unrealistic Social Standards**

    - Society often presents “perfect” images—perfect bodies, perfect jobs, perfect lives. Comparing yourself to these can lead to feeling unworthy.
    - **Solution**: Challenge these images. Remind yourself that they are often edited or only show one side of a person’s life. Focus on your own growth.
3. **Harsh Self-Judgment**
    - Some people treat themselves worse than they ever would treat a friend, calling themselves names or replaying mistakes over and over.
    - **Solution**: Ask, “Would I say this to a friend?” If not, do not say it to yourself. Practice using kinder language in your thoughts.
4. **Ignoring Achievements**
    - You might brush off what you have done well by saying, “Anybody could do that.”
    - **Solution**: Make a habit of pausing to acknowledge small and big successes, even if they feel normal. Over time, you recognize your abilities.

Self-Worth vs. Ego

Sometimes, people worry that having a sense of worth will turn into arrogance. But self-worth is not about seeing yourself as better than others. It is about seeing yourself as worthy of respect, just like all human beings. Arrogance usually involves putting others down to feel good. True self-worth allows you to respect yourself without lowering anyone else.

Real-Life Stories of Rebuilding Self-Worth

1. **Case: Mia, the Overworker**
    - **Background**: Mia believed her value depended on her job performance. She took on extra shifts, rarely rested, and felt anxious if she was not the top performer.
    - **Turnaround**: She started therapy after suffering burnout. Her counselor helped her see she was valuable even when not working.

Mia began taking weekends off and realized her friendships and family life improved. Over time, she saw herself as deserving of rest and not just as a worker.

2. **Case: Daniel, the People-Pleaser**
    - **Background**: Daniel grew up with critical parents who only praised him if he excelled in every task. As an adult, he tried to make everyone happy, even strangers.
    - **Turnaround**: With guidance from a friend, Daniel began saying "no" to requests that he could not handle. Each time, he felt guilty but also noticed he had more time for himself. Eventually, he discovered that true friends respected his boundaries, and he no longer depended on being useful to everyone for his sense of worth.
3. **Case: Ava, the Chronic Self-Critic**
    - **Background**: Ava was teased in school. She internalized these taunts, calling herself ugly or stupid in her mind. She avoided social events.
    - **Turnaround**: She challenged her self-talk by writing down her negative phrases and refuting them with evidence. She also took up a creative hobby that she enjoyed, which boosted her sense of capability. Over time, the negative labels lost strength, and she started feeling comfortable going to small gatherings again.

How to Keep Self-Worth Steady

Building self-worth is not a one-time event. It is an ongoing process of nurturing a new view of yourself. Here are steps to keep it steady:

1. **Regular Reflection**
    - Spend a few minutes weekly asking, "What did I do well this week? How did I treat myself?" Keep track in a journal to spot progress.
2. **Healthy Boundaries**
    - Remember the link between boundaries and self-worth. Enforcing fair limits in your personal and professional life helps you remember that your needs matter.
3. **Avoid Overload**

    - Taking on too many tasks or responsibilities can lead to feeling overwhelmed, which can weaken your sense of worth if you start blaming yourself for exhaustion or mistakes.
4. **Learn From Mistakes**
    - When errors happen, see them as lessons, not proof of your worth. Ask, "What can I learn here?" Then move forward.
5. **Support System**
    - Stay connected to friends, groups, or counselors who reinforce your sense of worth rather than tearing it down. If you find a relationship draining, re-evaluate it.

Lesser-Known Tips for Strengthening Self-Worth

1. **Use Everyday Tasks as Reminders**
    - Pair a daily activity, like brushing your teeth, with a short self-worth statement: "I take care of myself because I matter." This tiny habit can reinforce your sense of value.
2. **Create a Personal Motto**
    - A short phrase like "I am more than my mistakes" or "I am allowed to grow" can be repeated when you feel self-doubt creeping in.
3. **Record Praise**
    - If someone says something kind about you, write it down. When you feel low, read over these positive words to remind yourself that others recognize your worth too.
4. **Focus on Progress, Not Outcome**
    - If you only feel worthy when you win or succeed, your self-worth will rise and fall. Instead, notice if you are improving or learning new skills, which holds value regardless of the final result.

Addressing Self-Worth Setbacks

It is common to have days or weeks when negative thoughts return, especially if you face new challenges or triggers. Here is how to handle setbacks:

- **Acknowledge the Dip**: Recognize that you are feeling lower about yourself.

- **Review Your Tools**: Return to journaling, positive statements, or speaking with a supportive friend.
- **Seek Additional Help**: If the setback is strong, a therapist or group can offer further guidance.
- **Avoid Self-Shaming**: Do not criticize yourself for sliding backward; healing is an ongoing process.

How Strong Self-Worth Boosts Inner Child Healing

When your inner child sees that you carry yourself with basic dignity, it learns a new reality: "We are not worthless." This can mend old wounds from times when you were told you did not matter. Over time, your adult actions and attitudes can provide proof to the younger you that things have changed. You can show kindness toward yourself even if you do not always succeed, which undoes the messages of the past.

Conclusion of Chapter 11

Self-worth is the bedrock of a stable and fulfilling life. It means you do not need to base your sense of value on external events or other people's opinions. Instead, you know you deserve respect just by existing. While childhood experiences may have harmed this sense of worth, you can rebuild it through honesty, daily habits, and mindful choices about whom you surround yourself with. Each step you take—no matter how small—sends a signal to your inner child that you are indeed valuable.

In the next chapter, we will explore the idea of enjoying simple play, which helps many adults reconnect with the lighthearted side of their inner child. This play not only offers relaxation but also supports the sense of joy and worth that you have been working on in previous chapters.

CHAPTER 12: ENJOYING SIMPLE PLAY

Introduction

Play is often thought of as something only children do. But adults also benefit from playful activities. When you engage in simple, fun moments, you lighten your mood, reduce stress, and grant yourself a break from constant tasks. For the inner child, play can be a powerful way to feel safe and free. If your younger self was robbed of normal childhood experiences—perhaps due to family problems, early responsibilities, or emotional hardships—introducing play now can help fill that gap.

In this chapter, we will explore why play is helpful for emotional healing, how to find types of play that fit your interests, and ways to bring small moments of fun into your daily life. We will also look at common barriers that stop adults from letting themselves relax and enjoy playful moments.

Why Play Matters for Healing

1. **Stress Relief**
   During play, your mind focuses on a simple activity that does not carry heavy expectations. This shift can ease tension and help you return to daily tasks with more calmness.
2. **Emotional Expression**
   Some forms of play, like drawing or making up silly stories, allow you to express feelings in a creative way. This can help release trapped emotions.
3. **Connecting with Others**
   Group play—like board games or casual sports—can foster social bonds. You share laughter, learn cooperation, and remember that interaction can be fun, not just duty.
4. **Inner Child Nurturing**
   Many children heal from stress or sadness through play. For the adult who is still dealing with childhood wounds, play offers a second chance to experience the lightheartedness that might have been missed.

Different Kinds of Play

1. **Artistic Play**
   Activities like painting, coloring books, or doodling on paper can bring a sense of freedom. You do not need to be an artist; the act of creating is the key.
2. **Physical Play**
   Simple sports, dancing around your living room, or playful walks can give a childlike rush of energy. Physical movement tied to fun often boosts mood.
3. **Imaginative Play**
   Role-playing a character in a game, making up short stories, or daydreaming about fun scenarios can awaken your creative side.
4. **Group Games**
   Card games, board games, or simple video games with friends or family can spark laughter and teamwork. The social aspect can reinforce bonds.
5. **Nature Play**
   Skipping stones at a lake, building sandcastles at the beach, or collecting interesting rocks on a hike can bring a carefree feeling.

Common Barriers to Adult Play and How to Overcome Them

1. **Feeling Embarrassed**
   - Many adults think play is childish or silly. They fear judgment from others if they start coloring in a book or rolling on the grass.
   - **Solution**: Remind yourself that play reduces stress and can enhance creativity. Try playful acts in private at first if you feel too self-conscious, then expand as you get more comfortable.
2. **Time Constraints**
   - Busy schedules can lead people to feel they have no time for fun.
   - **Solution**: Start small. Even ten minutes of a playful activity can boost your mood. Schedule it like any other appointment until it becomes a habit.
3. **Perfectionism**
   - You might believe you can only do an activity if you are “good” at it. For instance, you might avoid art because you think you cannot draw.

    - **Solution**: Shift your focus from results to the process. You do not have to paint a masterpiece; you just need to enjoy the act of painting.
4. **Guilt**
    - Some adults feel guilty when not being "productive." They think leisure is a waste of time.
    - **Solution**: Remember that rest and play improve mental health, which in turn can help you be more productive later. It is an investment in well-being, not a waste.

How Simple Play Helps the Inner Child

If you imagine a small child who rarely got to laugh or explore because of stressful home conditions, you can see why playful moments now might act like emotional medicine. By allowing yourself to run around a field, play a harmless prank with a friend, or laugh at goofy jokes, you give that younger side of you a taste of what it missed. These bits of fun show the inner child that life can be more than just worry or duty.

Steps to Start Incorporating Play

1. Make a Fun List

Take five minutes to list playful or creative things you liked as a kid or have always wanted to try. This might include flying a kite, building a puzzle, or even something like blowing bubbles.

2. Pick One Activity Weekly

Choose one item from your list and set aside a small block of time for it. Do not wait until you "feel like it." Commit to it as you would any important task.

3. Experiment Without Judgment

Approach each activity as a test run. Let go of expectations about being "good" at it. Simply explore how it feels.

4. Invite Others, If You Like

If you feel comfortable, include a friend or family member. Shared fun can strengthen bonds and remind you that it is okay to be lighthearted with people you trust.

5. Adjust as Needed

If an activity does not bring joy or feels too forced, try something else. The goal is to find forms of play that genuinely spark a sense of freedom.

Practical Examples of Adult Play

1. **Midday Dance Break**
   - Set an alarm for a random time during the day. When it goes off, play a favorite upbeat song and dance for the length of that track—maybe 3 or 4 minutes. Allow yourself to move however you like.
2. **Coloring for Grownups**
   - Some people enjoy using coloring books designed for adults, with intricate patterns. You can do it for 10 minutes after a stressful meeting. The repetitive motion can be calming.
3. **Outdoor Hide-and-Seek with Kids (or Playful Adults)**
   - If you have children, nieces, nephews, or playful friends, organize a short game of hide-and-seek in a safe outdoor area. Even 15 minutes can remind you how it feels to laugh and run freely.
4. **Cooking as Play**
   - Instead of seeing cooking as a chore, try making a silly themed meal. Shape the food in interesting ways or create fun names for the dishes. This breaks the routine and sparks creative thinking.
5. **Short Skits or Puppet Shows**
   - If you have a couple of small puppets or stuffed toys, invent a quick skit. It might feel strange at first, but it can quickly become a joyful act.

The Mental Health Benefits of Play

1. **Reduced Stress Hormones**
   Activities you find fun can lower cortisol (a stress hormone) in your body, leading to a calmer state.
2. **Improved Mood**
   Laughter or gentle physical movement during play can trigger endorphins—chemicals in the brain that enhance mood and help you feel more relaxed.
3. **Better Focus**
   Play breaks can refresh your mind, making it easier to return to tasks with new energy or insight.
4. **Emotional Resilience**
   Regular exposure to low-pressure fun moments helps you face challenges with a lighter outlook. You remember that life has pockets of joy even when times are tough.

Dealing with Self-Conscious Feelings

It is natural to feel awkward if you have not played in a long time. You might worry about appearing childish or unprofessional. But consider:

- **Privacy Is an Option**: Begin alone in your home if you feel too shy to play around others.
- **Choose People Who Support You**: If you do want to play with others, pick those who do not judge easily.
- **Accept Awkwardness**: Feeling silly is not harmful. In fact, learning to laugh at yourself can be a form of emotional release.

Linking Simple Play to Other Healing Steps

Play does not stand alone in healing. It complements other steps like self-worth building, handling shame, and trusting your thoughts. When you engage in playful moments, you challenge the idea that you must always be serious or perfect. You also provide evidence to your inner child that you are willing to enjoy life rather than just survive it.

Real-Life Stories of Playful Healing

1. **Case: Brian's Balloon Game**
   - **Situation**: Brian felt constant stress in his demanding job. He realized he had not done anything playful in years.
   - **Action**: He remembered enjoying balloon volleyball as a kid—hitting a balloon around a room without letting it touch the floor. He decided to buy a pack of balloons and do this for 10 minutes when he got home each evening.
   - **Result**: At first, Brian felt foolish batting a balloon alone in his living room. But he soon found himself laughing. His stress eased, and he even invited his roommate to join, leading to shared fun.
2. **Case: Selena's Weekly Craft Night**
   - **Situation**: Selena felt disconnected from her inner child. She used to love making friendship bracelets at summer camp but had abandoned any kind of crafts as she grew older.
   - **Action**: She set up a weekly craft night, inviting a friend who also enjoyed making things by hand. They tried bead bracelets, paper flowers, and silly clay figures.
   - **Result**: These craft sessions became a highlight of Selena's week. She noticed she slept better afterward, and her sense of creativity bled into other areas of her life.
3. **Case: Omar's Improv Meetups**
   - **Situation**: Omar was shy and struggled with social fear. A counselor suggested he try something playful in a group setting to build confidence.
   - **Action**: Omar found a local improv group that welcomed beginners. He feared judgment at first, but the group was supportive. They treated mistakes as part of the fun.
   - **Result**: Omar began to realize he could make silly jokes or scenarios without being ridiculed. Over time, his social anxiety dropped, and he even made a few new friends.

Simple Play Exercises

Exercise 1: Bubble Break

1. Buy or make a small bottle of bubble solution (soap + water).
2. Once a day, head outside (or a room that is easy to clean) and blow bubbles for a few minutes.
3. Watch them float, pop them if you like, and enjoy the simple magic of it.

Exercise 2: Art Time Challenge

1. Set a timer for 15 minutes.
2. Draw, paint, or create something without stopping. No erasing or perfecting—just let your hand move.
3. Stop when the timer dings, and look at what you made. Whether it is a scribble or a mini-masterpiece, it served as a playful outlet.

Exercise 3: Silly Storytelling

1. Either alone or with a friend, pick a random topic (like a lost turtle, a space bakery, or a giant carrot) and invent a short, silly story on the spot.
2. Let your mind roam free without worrying about logic.
3. If you do this with someone else, take turns adding sentences to build the story.

Adding Play to Your Routine

1. **Morning Routines**
    - Before diving into the day's responsibilities, take a few minutes to do something lighthearted: a short dance, a quick doodle, or a funny face in the mirror.
2. **Work Breaks**
    - Instead of scrolling aimlessly on your phone, try a playful mini-activity—like a small puzzle or a quick stretch that feels like a game.

3. **Evening Wind-Down**
    - If you live with others, take a few minutes to toss a soft ball around or play a short game. If alone, you might prefer a single-player puzzle or coloring time.
4. **Weekends**
    - Choose at least one playful outing or project each weekend. It could be a walk in a nearby park where you take silly photos or a quick session of a new hobby.

Handling Resistance to Play

If you find yourself resisting these activities or feeling they are "too childish," remember:

- **You Decide the Activity Level**: You do not have to jump up and down for hours. Even a lighthearted 5-minute puzzle can be enough.
- **No One Is Keeping Score**: The goal is not to reach a specific target or impress anyone. It is to relax and awaken a sense of fun.
- **Old Messages Might Return**: You may hear an inner voice saying, "Stop fooling around." Acknowledge that voice, but gently proceed with your chosen activity.

How Play Interacts with Other Chapters' Lessons

- **Self-Kindness (Chapter 4)**: Play helps you be gentle with yourself, reminding you that you deserve leisure.
- **Trusting Your Own Thoughts (Chapter 5)**: You might have an impulse to try something silly. Play allows you to trust that impulse without overthinking.
- **Breaking Harmful Patterns (Chapter 6)**: If you usually spend free time worrying or doing chores, play challenges that pattern with a fresh option.
- **Shame and Guilt (Chapter 8)**: Harmless play can counter the idea that you are not allowed to have fun. It shows you are worthy of relaxation.
- **Self-Worth (Chapter 11)**: Engaging in playful moments can reinforce the idea that your time and joy have value.

Lesser-Known Insights on Play (Extra Useful Information)

1. **Use Senses You Rarely Engage**
    - If you typically work on a computer (visual, mental focus), try a play activity that uses smell or touch, like kneading dough or exploring fragrant soaps, to expand your sensory experience.
2. **Small Shared Rituals**
    - If you live with someone, create a tiny daily or weekly game. For example, "Every Friday night, we each do a 1-minute comedic act for each other." This fosters connection and keeps things light.
3. **Incorporate Mindfulness**
    - While playing, notice small details: the colors of your crayons, the texture of the ball, the breeze on your face. This level of focus deepens the relaxation effect.
4. **Use Nostalgia**
    - Revisit a game you played as a child (jacks, a simple video game, marbles) if it holds no painful memories. Sometimes, nostalgia can spark extra warmth and contentment.

What to Do If Play Brings Up Sadness

In some cases, trying to play can remind you of lost childhood moments or painful memories. This is normal. Do not force yourself to push past overwhelming sadness if it arises. Instead:

- **Pause and Breathe**: Take a break from the play activity.
- **Acknowledge the Feeling**: You can say, "I feel sad because I missed out on this as a child."
- **Seek Comfort**: Talk to a supportive friend, or write down your feelings.
- **Try a Different Play Style**: Some forms of play might be too closely linked to past hurts. Explore another type that feels safer or new.

Over time, you may find that you can gently return to the activity once the sadness is less intense.

Keeping Play in Your Healing Journey

As with other tools in this book, simple play is not a magic fix. It is one piece of a larger approach to healing your inner child. Still, maintaining regular moments of fun can help balance the deeper emotional work you do. If you ever feel overwhelmed by confronting old wounds or tackling big life changes, a few playful minutes can remind you that life includes lightness as well.

Conclusion of Chapter 12

Enjoying simple play is one of the most direct ways to reach your inner child and soothe old pain. By engaging in fun tasks—whether creative, physical, or social—you offer yourself a sense of freedom that might have been missing in earlier years. This sense of fun fosters lower stress, better mood, and a gentle boost in self-worth. Overcoming embarrassment or the belief that play is unproductive can take time, but the benefits for your emotional health are significant.

From small solo activities to playful group games, there are countless ways to open the door to this lighter side of life. As you continue through the later chapters, remember to keep a playful spirit in mind. Next, we will look at how creative exercises can deepen your healing, building on the theme of playful exploration and expression covered here.

CHAPTER 13: CREATIVE EXERCISES

Introduction

Creativity is an outlet for feelings, thoughts, and ideas that may not always come out in everyday conversations. It goes beyond painting or drawing; it can include writing, crafting, music, and many other forms of expression. When people tap into creative exercises, they often find it easier to release stress, clarify problems, and connect with feelings they did not realize they had.

For someone healing their inner child, creative exercises can serve as gentle gateways to emotions that might have been buried for a long time. In this chapter, we will explore the importance of creativity for emotional growth, various types of creative outlets, and practical ways to start. We will address common roadblocks—like worrying about talent or time—and give detailed methods to include creativity in your daily life. By the end of this chapter, you will have a collection of strategies to bring creativity into your personal healing process.

Why Creativity Supports Healing

1. **Opens the Door to Hidden Feelings**
   Sometimes, words are not enough to capture what you feel. A simple sketch, a poem, or a few musical notes can convey an emotion in a deeper way. When you make something with your hands or mind, you give yourself space to process experiences that might otherwise remain locked away.
2. **Reduces Stress**
   Many creative tasks—like coloring, crafting, or writing—have a calming effect on the nervous system. They can distract you from worries and help your mind shift to a more relaxed focus. This can lower stress hormones, providing relief from daily tensions.
3. **Builds Self-Trust**
   Exploring new creative paths allows you to try ideas without harsh judgment. The more you trust your ability to create something, the more you strengthen self-belief. Even small creative wins—like finishing a

simple drawing—send a message to your mind that you can handle new challenges.

4. **Empowers the Inner Child**
   Children often express themselves through play and art. If your childhood lacked chances for free expression, creative exercises now can give that younger side of you the approval it did not receive before. When you write a silly story or paint with bright colors, you might sense a joyful relief that helps mend old emotional wounds.

Common Misunderstandings About Creativity

1. **"I'm Not an Artist"**
   Creativity is not limited to people who call themselves artists. It includes many everyday forms of expression—like rearranging your room, doodling on a scrap of paper, or writing short notes in a diary.
2. **"I Don't Have the Right Supplies"**
   You do not need fancy tools or a big budget. A simple pen and paper can be enough to release powerful emotions. Creative thinking can happen anywhere, with whatever materials you have at hand.
3. **"Creativity Takes Too Much Time"**
   Even a few minutes of creative effort can boost your mood. Whether it is a five-minute freewriting session or a short photo walk, small bursts of creativity can fit into a busy schedule.
4. **"It Has to Be Good"**
   The goal of creative exercises for emotional healing is not to produce a masterpiece. The focus is on the process—what you discover, feel, and learn while doing it. Mistakes, smudges, and uneven stitches can all be part of the meaningful experience.

Types of Creative Outlets

1. **Visual Art**
   - **Sketching or Drawing**: This can range from simple pencil doodles to more detailed sketches.
   - **Coloring**: You can use coloring books or just fill blank pages with shapes and shades that appeal to you.

    - **Painting**: Acrylic, watercolor, or even finger painting all allow color and texture to come alive on a surface.
2. **Writing**
    - **Journaling**: Writing about your day, your hopes, or your reflections can clarify thoughts.
    - **Poetry**: Short, informal poems can capture feelings that are hard to explain in normal sentences.
    - **Short Fiction**: Inventing characters and small plots might help you explore personal themes in a less direct way.
3. **Musical Expression**
    - **Playing an Instrument**: Even if you are not skilled, strumming a guitar or tapping on a keyboard can be freeing.
    - **Singing**: You can hum tunes or sing simple songs to release emotional tension.
    - **Rhythms and Beats**: Clapping or drumming on a table can also serve as a fun, stress-relieving activity.
4. **Crafts and Hands-On Projects**
    - **Knitting or Crocheting**: Repetitive motions can calm the mind, similar to a meditative practice.
    - **Collage or Scrapbooking**: Cutting and arranging images or words can help you visually piece together parts of yourself.
    - **Clay or Play Dough**: Molding shapes engages your sense of touch, which can be very grounding.
5. **Movement and Body-Based Creativity**
    - **Dance or Simple Movement**: Letting your body sway to music, without worrying about steps, can help free up feelings.
    - **Body Tracing**: Outlining your hand or foot on paper, then coloring it, can be a symbolic way to connect with your physical self.
    - **Improvised Drama**: Acting out short scenes or facial expressions in front of a mirror can help release tension.

How to Begin a Creative Practice

1. **Set a Non-Judgment Rule**
   Before starting, decide that you will not judge the result of your creativity. If a picture looks messy, let it be. If your story seems silly, that is okay. The point is to experiment and learn about yourself.

2. **Gather Simple Supplies**
   Put together a small "creativity kit" with items like paper, pens, crayons, or any craft materials you have lying around. Having them ready removes the barrier of searching for supplies each time.
3. **Choose a Comfortable Space**
   Find a spot where you feel safe to try things without interruption. It could be a corner of your living room, a kitchen table, or a small outdoor area.
4. **Schedule Small Blocks of Time**
   Aim for short sessions, like 10–15 minutes a few times a week. You can always extend the time if you feel inspired.
5. **Track Your Feelings**
   After each creative session, jot down a few words about how you felt during and after the activity. Over time, you may see patterns indicating which activities reduce stress or bring insights.

Overcoming Creative Blocks

1. **Fear of Making Mistakes**
   - **Tip**: Give yourself permission to produce flawed work. Mistakes can lead to unexpected outcomes that reveal new possibilities.
2. **Too Many Ideas**
   - **Tip**: Write down any ideas quickly in a notebook, then pick one to focus on. You can return to the others later.
3. **No Ideas**
   - **Tip**: Try a prompt. For art, pick a theme like "my favorite shape." For writing, choose a random word and build a story around it.
4. **Comparison to Others**
   - **Tip**: If you find yourself comparing your creations to those of professional artists or writers, remember that you are doing this for emotional expression, not competition.
5. **Lack of Motivation**
   - **Tip**: Start with something very small, like drawing a single shape or writing one sentence. Sometimes, just starting can spark more energy.

Linking Creative Exercises with Inner Child Work

Your inner child is the part of you that learned how to see the world at a young age. Creative play can speak directly to that part, bypassing the guarded adult mind. Here are ways to connect your exercises to inner child healing:

1. **Childhood Themes**
   Create an image or short story around a theme from your early years—like a favorite toy, a memorable place, or a small event that stood out. This can help you process lingering emotions tied to that memory.
2. **Symbolic Artwork**
   Use shapes, colors, or images that represent how you felt as a child. For instance, if you felt lonely, you might draw a small figure surrounded by empty space. This can make hidden feelings more visible.
3. **Writing Letters**
   Write a letter from your present self to your younger self, or vice versa. Do not worry about spelling or style. Just let the words flow, even if they come out scattered.
4. **Storytelling**
   If you have a strong painful memory, try re-imagining it as a story where you give your younger self some help or protect them from harm. This is not about rewriting history, but about offering comfort and acceptance that your child side might have needed.
5. **Celebrating Simple Achievements**
   After finishing any small creative piece, reflect on the fact that you completed it. This sense of accomplishment can reassure your younger self that you can bring ideas to life.

Real-Life Examples

1. **Case: Leah and Memory Collage**
   - **Situation**: Leah felt stuck with old regrets about her childhood. She found it hard to talk about them directly.
   - **Creative Approach**: She gathered magazines, newspapers, and old pictures, then cut out images and words that seemed to represent her early feelings—images of locked doors, silent faces, and a single bright flower. She glued them on a poster in a free-form way.

    - **Outcome**: Seeing the collage helped Leah recognize which aspects of her past made her feel most trapped. She later used it to guide discussions in therapy, finding ways to address those locked-door sensations.
2. **Case: Marcus and Clay Shapes**
    - **Situation**: Marcus felt numb whenever he tried to speak about childhood fears.
    - **Creative Approach**: A friend suggested that Marcus try working with air-dry clay. He began making simple abstract forms—some looked like wavy lines, others like jagged shapes. He realized that certain shapes came to him when he was recalling specific events.
    - **Outcome**: Holding or pressing the clay allowed Marcus to release tension physically. Over time, he linked certain shapes with feelings of anger or sadness. This made it easier to admit those feelings existed, instead of ignoring them.
3. **Case: Tasha and a Song Journal**
    - **Situation**: Tasha loved music as a child but was told she was too loud. She stopped singing to avoid getting in trouble at home.
    - **Creative Approach**: She decided to keep a "song journal." Each day, she wrote a short phrase about how she felt—like "Today I'm tired but hopeful"—and then tried to sing that line in any tune that popped into her head.
    - **Outcome**: Tasha discovered that singing her feelings, even in a quiet voice, made her days feel lighter. This small act reminded her that her voice mattered. She gained the courage to join a casual choir group after a few months.

Practical Exercises for Creative Expression

Exercise 1: Freewriting for 5 Minutes

1. Grab a pen and paper.
2. Set a timer for 5 minutes.
3. Write continuously without stopping. Do not worry if your sentences make sense or if your spelling is correct. Just let words flow.
4. When the timer rings, read over what you wrote. Notice any themes or surprises.
5. If it feels right, highlight a sentence or phrase that stands out to you.

Exercise 2: Color-and-Feel

1. Pick at least three colored pencils or markers that you feel drawn to.
2. On a blank paper, assign each color to an emotion. For example, blue might be calm, red might be frustration, and green might be hope.
3. Scribble or draw shapes on the page, letting each color represent how you feel in that moment.
4. See if the size or intensity of each color reveals something about your mood. If you notice you used a lot of red, it might indicate you have unaddressed tension.

Exercise 3: Object Transformation

1. Think of a small object you see every day (like a spoon, a key, or a shoe).
2. Write a short paragraph or create a simple sketch showing that object as something magical, funny, or completely different from what it is. For example, imagine the spoon is a tiny boat or the key can open hidden doors to new worlds.
3. Let your mind play with the possibilities. This can be a fun way to spark creative thinking.

Lesser-Known Techniques for Creativity (Extra Useful Insights)

1. **Micro-Moments of Art**
    - If you are busy, try micro-moments. For example, while waiting in line at a store, quickly doodle a shape on a small notepad. These tiny bursts can keep your creative flow alive.
2. **Use Found Materials**
    - Instead of buying new supplies, look around your home for old magazines, leftover yarn, or even small stones from outdoors. Turning random items into art can spur resourceful thinking.
3. **Multi-Sensory Creation**
    - Combine two senses in one activity. For instance, paint while listening to music that matches the mood you want to capture. Or write a poem based on a scent that evokes childhood memories.
4. **Creative Buddy System**

    - Find a friend who also wants to boost creativity. Share your small pieces with each other once a week. This adds accountability and can expand your perspectives.
5. **Emotion Playlists**
    - If you like music, create short playlists for specific moods—like sadness, excitement, or nostalgia. Listen to them while creating art or writing, letting the music guide your expressions.

Addressing Doubts and Setbacks

- **"I'm Bored With This"**: It might be that you need a new creative approach. Try switching from drawing to writing, or from writing to clay.
- **"I Feel Too Exposed"**: If creative work brings up intense emotions, take smaller steps or seek support from a counselor. Do not push yourself too hard too soon.
- **"I Can't Find Time Anymore"**: Life can get hectic. Try to include creative breaks into routine tasks. For instance, doodle on a napkin while on a phone call or hum a song while doing chores.
- **"No One Cares About My Art"**: Remember that this is primarily for you, not for external praise. If sharing it is stressful, you can keep it private or show it only to someone you trust.

How Creativity Links to Other Healing Steps

- **Self-Worth**: Seeing that you can create something unique, even if simple, can raise your sense of value.
- **Handling Shame**: Creative expression can help you let out feelings of shame in a safe, constructive way.
- **Trusting Your Thoughts**: Each time you act on a creative idea, you reinforce the belief that your mind's sparks are valid.
- **Boundaries**: Sometimes you need to set aside "do not disturb" time to create. This boundary respects your need for personal space and fosters self-care.

Practical Tips for Long-Term Creative Growth

1. **Keep a Creativity Journal**
   - Jot down ideas, rough sketches, or lines of poetry as they come to you. Look back on it once a month to see how you have grown.
2. **Try Group Workshops**
   - If you feel ready, join a local or online workshop. Learning alongside others can build skills and confidence.
3. **Challenge Yourself Periodically**
   - Every now and then, pick a project that feels slightly out of your comfort zone. This may open new doors in your self-awareness and emotional depth.
4. **Celebrate Completions**
   - When you finish a piece—be it a small poem or a craft—pause and acknowledge the effort. Give yourself a pat on the back for doing something creative.
5. **Stay Flexible**
   - The form of creativity that works for you might change over time. Maybe you start with painting but later shift to simple photography. Follow where your curiosity leads you.

Conclusion of Chapter 13

Creative exercises are powerful tools for anyone seeking emotional relief, self-discovery, and a deeper connection with their inner child. By giving yourself permission to explore, you unlock parts of yourself that plain conversation might not reveal. Whether through art, writing, music, or crafts, creativity can help you feel more alive and aware of your own feelings.

Remember, your goal is not perfection. It is about learning who you are, what you feel, and how you can express that in a safe, friendly way. As you continue your healing path, let creativity be a companion that gently encourages growth. In the next chapter, we will move on to releasing past anger—another major issue for many people whose inner child has carried old wounds. While creativity can also help with anger, Chapter 14 will offer more direct ways to recognize and let go of that burden.

CHAPTER 14: RELEASING PAST ANGER

Introduction

Anger is often called a "secondary emotion." It can appear when you feel hurt, betrayed, or disrespected. It can also arise if you have unmet needs or unresolved events from childhood. Many people struggle with anger they have carried for years, sometimes not even knowing where it started. For someone working on their inner child, past anger can show up in bursts or simmer quietly under the surface, leading to anxiety, depression, or strained relationships.

In this chapter, we will explore why anger from the past can linger, how it affects both the mind and body, and how to release it in healthy ways. We will cover strategies such as acknowledging triggers, expressing anger without harm, and rebuilding trust in yourself so that you do not stay locked in old resentments. By understanding the roots of your anger and learning constructive steps to let it go, you can open the door to inner calm and better emotional balance.

Why Does Old Anger Stay?

1. **Unresolved Conflicts**
   If you had fights or conflicts in the past that were never settled, the anger can remain. You might replay the event in your mind, wishing you had said or done something different.
2. **Suppression**
   Some families or cultures discourage showing anger. You might have learned to stuff it down, only for it to reappear later when triggered by something that seems small on the surface.
3. **Lack of Emotional Safety**
   As a child, if you were not allowed to speak up or if you faced punishment for expressing any displeasure, you might still carry that frustrated energy. It sits in the background, waiting to erupt in other situations.
4. **Distorted Self-Blame**
   Sometimes, anger at others turns inward if you were taught that feeling mad was bad. Instead of directing anger where it belongs, you might feel shame or guilt, adding to your emotional load.

The Impact of Old Anger

1. **Stress on the Body**
   High levels of anger can keep your body in a state of tension, raising stress hormones that can affect your sleep, heart rate, and overall health.
2. **Damaged Relationships**
   When anger is unresolved, it can leak out at unexpected times. You might snap at friends or family for minor reasons, leaving them confused or hurt.
3. **Clouded Judgment**
   Anger can narrow your focus, making it hard to see situations clearly. You might interpret neutral comments as attacks or find it difficult to stay calm when making decisions.
4. **Emotional Exhaustion**
   Constant anger, even if it is under the surface, can leave you feeling drained and less able to enjoy daily life.

Recognizing the Signs of Old Anger

- **Recurring Thoughts**: You revisit a particular memory of hurt or injustice, and it still stirs strong feelings.
- **Tension in the Body**: Certain triggers—like a tone of voice or a phrase—make your muscles tighten or your heart rate spike.
- **Overreaction to Minor Events**: You notice that a small annoyance sets you off more than seems normal.
- **Persistent Irritability**: You feel edgy much of the time, and little things seem to get under your skin easily.

Steps to Let Go of Old Anger

Step 1: Admit It Exists

It may sound basic, but many people deny or downplay their anger. You might say, "I'm just annoyed," or "I don't care," when in fact you feel deeply hurt or resentful. Being honest is the first major move toward release.

Step 2: Identify the Source

Sometimes it is clear where the anger started—perhaps an event like bullying or a betrayal. Other times, you might need to do some introspection. Journaling or talking with a counselor can help you piece together connections.

Step 3: Explore Safe Outlets

Once you admit you are angry, you need a safe method to express it. This can include writing an unsent letter, speaking out loud in private, or using a punching pillow to release tension. The idea is to let the emotion out in a way that does not harm you or anyone else.

Step 4: Check for Underlying Feelings

Anger often covers up more vulnerable emotions like sadness, fear, or longing. Once the anger has a chance to be released, you might discover a layer of grief or hurt underneath that also needs attention.

Step 5: Consider Forgiveness or Closure

Forgiveness does not mean forgetting or letting someone off the hook if they acted badly. It means deciding not to carry the weight of that anger any longer. If direct closure with the person is not possible, you can still find internal closure through self-reflection and self-care.

Methods for Releasing Anger Safely

1. **Writing Unsent Letters**
   - Write a letter to the person or situation that caused the anger. Pour out all your thoughts. You do not need to send it. The act of writing can help you organize and release the built-up feelings.
2. **Physical Outlet**
   - Activities like brisk walking, dancing, or light exercise can burn off the energy that anger creates. Some people find hitting a pillow or using a stress ball helpful, as long as they do so mindfully, without hurting themselves.
3. **Verbal Release in Private**

    - Find a private space, like your car or a room, and speak out loud about what angers you. Allow your voice to reflect how you feel. This might feel awkward at first, but it can be very freeing.
4. **Creative Expression**
    - Draw or paint shapes and colors that match your anger's intensity. Use bright, harsh lines or deep shades if that suits your mood. This merges the creative approach from the previous chapter with anger release.
5. **Therapy or Counseling**
    - A professional can guide you through deeper anger release techniques, especially if you have experienced major trauma or if your anger feels overwhelming.

Linking Anger Release to the Inner Child

The younger you might have felt helpless or fearful when facing aggression, neglect, or unfair treatment. Releasing anger as an adult can be a way to defend that child who never had a chance to speak. This involves:

- **Visualizing the Child**: Picture your younger self beside you while you vent anger in a safe way. Remind them that it is now okay to be upset about what happened.
- **Offering Reassurance**: After releasing anger, take a moment to speak kindly to that child, affirming that they are safe and not at fault.
- **Small Comforting Rituals**: You might follow an anger release session with a soothing activity—like wrapping yourself in a blanket or listening to calming music—to let the child inside feel supported.

Real-Life Examples of Releasing Anger

1. **Case: Aria and Family Arguments**
    - **Situation**: Aria grew up in a household where shouting was common and her opinions were dismissed. She often felt overlooked.
    - **Action**: As an adult, she noticed she would snap at colleagues for minor mistakes. This confused her and strained her work

environment. Through reflection, she realized she carried a lot of anger from childhood.

   - **Method**: Aria began writing letters addressed to her past family situations whenever she felt triggered at work. She then destroyed these letters or stored them away safely without sending them. This helped her channel the anger into words instead of lashing out.
   - **Outcome**: Over time, Aria felt lighter and found that she snapped less at coworkers. She also started setting boundaries with her family, calmly explaining that yelling was not acceptable to her anymore.

2. **Case: Neil and a Childhood Betrayal**
   - **Situation**: Neil's best friend in elementary school spread rumors about him. Neil never confronted him and acted like it did not bother him, but the anger stayed.
   - **Action**: As an adult, Neil realized he had trouble trusting new friends. He always expected them to betray him.
   - **Method**: With a counselor's help, he practiced a verbal release technique. He would sit alone and pretend he was speaking to that old friend, explaining how it felt to be betrayed.
   - **Outcome**: Although it was painful at first, Neil gradually released much of the bitterness. This allowed him to open up to people in the present, recognizing that not everyone would act like his former friend did.
3. **Case: Dina and Suppressed Feelings**
   - **Situation**: Dina was taught as a child that anger was unacceptable. She would be punished if she showed any sign of rage. By adulthood, she felt numb whenever she should have been angry.
   - **Action**: Dina started using physical outlets—like punching a pillow while telling herself it was okay to feel mad. At first, she cried instead of feeling anger, which revealed a layer of sadness.
   - **Outcome**: Over time, she discovered that once she allowed herself to feel anger, her general numbness decreased. She felt more alive and found a healthier way to address conflicts without fear.

Practical Exercises for Releasing Past Anger

Exercise 1: Drawing Your Anger

1. Take a blank sheet of paper and some pencils or markers.
2. Close your eyes for a moment, recall a situation that made you angry, and notice how your body feels.
3. Open your eyes and use shapes, lines, or colors that represent your anger. This might look messy, chaotic, or very intense.
4. When done, observe what you drew. You can reflect on the meaning of these shapes or colors.
5. If you want, you can tear it up or throw it away as a sign of letting go, or you can keep it as a reminder that you faced that anger safely.

Exercise 2: The Unsent Message

1. Write a text or email to the person or event that caused your anger.
2. Do not hold back—let your words express exactly how you feel.
3. Once finished, read it over. Notice if you feel relief or if any other emotions come up.
4. Delete it or save it in a private folder without sending. The important part is the expression, not the delivery.

Exercise 3: Body Scan for Trapped Tension

1. Find a quiet spot and sit comfortably.
2. Close your eyes and take a few slow breaths.
3. Scan your body from head to toe, looking for areas that feel tight or knotted.
4. When you find a tense spot, pause and ask yourself, "Is there anger stored here?"
5. Breathe into that area, and if you feel the need, let out a low sound or say a word that expresses frustration.
6. Continue until you have checked your whole body. This helps you notice physical signs of anger and release them bit by bit.

Lesser-Known Methods for Anger Release (Extra Useful Insights)

1. **Scribble Therapy**
   - Quickly scribble on a piece of paper with a pencil or pen, letting your hand move with the speed or intensity of your feeling. This can be surprisingly freeing.
2. **Ball Toss**
   - If you have someone you trust, toss a soft ball back and forth while talking about your frustrations. The physical act of throwing something safely can help release tension.
3. **Shower or Bath Expression**
   - Water can help calm the senses. While in the shower or bath, give yourself permission to speak or sigh about things that upset you. The sound of running water can also mask your words, adding privacy.
4. **Metaphorical Release**
   - Write your anger on a slip of paper and then place it in water, letting the ink blur, or burn it safely in a controlled setting. The visual act of it fading can assist the mind in letting go.
5. **Temperature and Texture**
   - Holding something cold or rough in your hands can ground you when anger spikes, shifting your focus from emotional heat to a sensory experience.

Self-Care After Anger Release

Releasing anger can be draining. It is wise to follow up with activities that restore calm and provide reassurance:

- **Drink Water or Tea**: Hydration can help settle your body's reaction to strong emotions.
- **Listen to Calming Music**: Soft tunes or nature sounds can bring your heart rate down.
- **Do a Comforting Activity**: This could be curling up in a blanket, reading a favorite book, or playing with a pet.
- **Reflect Gently**: Take a moment to note what you learned about yourself in that release. Did a deeper emotion surface? Did you feel relief?

Handling Roadblocks in Anger Release

- **Fear of Losing Control**: Some people worry that if they allow anger to show, it will become dangerous. That is why structured exercises (like writing or controlled physical outlets) are helpful.
- **Shame About Being Angry**: If you grew up thinking anger is wrong, it takes time to see that anger is a normal emotion that can be managed without harm.
- **Other People's Reactions**: You might worry about how friends or family respond when you begin to set limits or express anger. Clear communication can help them understand you are trying healthier methods.

How Releasing Past Anger Benefits the Inner Child

When your adult self deals with buried anger, you free that younger side of you from carrying it. It is like giving the child inside a voice—finally letting them say, "That was not fair!" or "I was hurt!" This can strengthen your sense of safety and lead to greater peace. You show the child inside that it is not weak to be angry; it is human. Handling anger well also reduces self-blame, because the child no longer thinks they were the cause of everything that went wrong.

Connection with Other Chapters' Themes

- **Self-Worth (Chapter 11)**: Letting go of blame or resentment can help you feel more worthy of respect and kindness.
- **Healthy Boundaries (Chapter 7)**: Sometimes anger points to boundary violations. Releasing anger can clarify where you need to set or reinforce those boundaries.
- **Handling Shame and Guilt (Chapter 8)**: Repressed anger can mix with shame. Facing anger openly can separate these emotions, allowing you to deal with guilt or shame on its own.

Final Thoughts on Long-Term Anger Management

Releasing anger from the past does not mean you will never feel mad again. Anger is a normal emotion that alerts you to possible dangers or unmet needs. But when you handle it step by step, you avoid becoming trapped in old resentments. You also learn to respond to new triggers with more calm, breaking the habit of overreaction.

Consider these ongoing tips for healthier anger management:

- **Regular Emotional Check-Ins**: Notice if tension is building so you can address it early.
- **Keep Practicing Outlets**: Keep up with letter writing, art, or other safe ways to let anger out before it grows.
- **Educate Yourself**: Books, workshops, or counseling on anger management can teach additional skills.
- **Stay Aware of Triggers**: If you know certain events or people spark your anger due to old wounds, prepare in advance or limit your exposure when possible.

Conclusion of Chapter 14

Old anger can feel like a weight you have carried for so long that you might not even notice its full impact. However, once you start recognizing it, expressing it in safe ways, and offering your younger self the care it lacked, you can gradually lighten that weight. Releasing anger is not about giving anyone a free pass for their wrongs; it is about freeing yourself from the damage of holding on.

By following the strategies outlined here—admitting anger, finding a safe outlet, and exploring deeper feelings beneath the rage—you strengthen your emotional health. You also show your inner child that it is finally safe to express what was once silenced. In the upcoming chapters, we will look at additional practices—such as self-reflection methods, setting clear goals, and developing self-coaching skills—that can support your ongoing healing and growth.

CHAPTER 15: PRACTICING SELF-REFLECTION

Introduction

Self-reflection is the act of looking at your thoughts, emotions, and actions in order to understand yourself better. Many of us move through life reacting to events without pausing to think about why we feel or act a certain way. However, self-reflection helps you see patterns, identify growth areas, and bring hidden motives to light. It can be one of the most powerful tools for anyone healing their inner child, as it allows you to notice emotional triggers, make sense of the past, and choose healthier responses for the future.

In this chapter, we will discuss the meaning of self-reflection, why it matters for emotional growth, and how to do it in a practical manner. We will also cover common misunderstandings about reflecting on yourself, along with tips to handle challenges like racing thoughts or discomfort. By the end, you should have a clear sense of why self-reflection is so crucial and how to include it in daily life without feeling overwhelmed.

Why Self-Reflection Matters

1. **Brings Unconscious Feelings to Awareness**
   Many feelings or responses are rooted in memories that you do not constantly think about. Self-reflection allows these deeper emotions to come forward, so you can understand them rather than just reacting blindly.
2. **Provides Insight into Patterns**
   Whether it is a habit of avoiding conflict or always apologizing first, repeating behaviors usually point to old beliefs or wounds. By noticing when these patterns arise, you can change them if they no longer serve you.
3. **Reduces Impulsive Responses**
   When you develop the habit of self-reflection, you learn to pause before

acting. Instead of rushing into an argument or shutting down completely, you can take a moment to see what you truly feel and want.

4. **Builds Self-Trust**
   As you reflect on your successes, struggles, and the motives behind your choices, you strengthen your connection with yourself. This can help you see your own thoughts as valid and worthy of attention.
5. **Supports Inner Child Healing**
   The child part of you may carry old hurts that shape your reactions today. Self-reflection is a safe way to visit those early experiences, feel what was not felt back then, and offer the care you once lacked.

What Self-Reflection Is (and Is Not)

- **It Is a Personal Exploration**: You are looking at your own mind, emotions, and behaviors without blaming others or seeking external validation.
- **It Is Not Self-Criticism**: Reflection is not about listing your faults. Though you may see areas for growth, the goal is understanding, not harsh judgment.
- **It Is Focused on Growth**: You want to see why you do certain things and learn from them, rather than staying stuck in old ways.
- **It Is Not Endless Overthinking**: While you do spend time looking at your inner world, you want to avoid spinning in circles of self-doubt. Reflection should lead to clarity and possible action, not constant rumination.

Signs You May Need More Self-Reflection

1. **Frequent Emotional Overreactions**: You lose your temper or become sad or anxious quickly, and later feel puzzled by your intensity.
2. **Repeating Conflicts**: You seem to have the same arguments or misunderstandings with people over and over.
3. **Feeling Disconnected**: You go through daily tasks on autopilot, feeling numb or detached from what you do.
4. **Lack of Direction**: You realize you do not know what you truly want out of situations or life in general.

5. **Difficulty Making Decisions**: You find it very hard to choose, possibly because you are out of touch with your core values.

Methods of Self-Reflection

1. **Journaling**
    - Keeping a journal is one of the most common ways to reflect. You can write about your day, your emotions, or specific events.
    - Over time, you might spot repeating patterns or triggers in your journal entries.
    - No fancy format is needed. A few lines each day can be very revealing.
2. **Guided Questions**
    - Asking yourself specific questions can spark deeper insight. Examples include:
        - "What did I feel strongly about today and why?"
        - "What do I wish I had done differently?"
        - "How did I speak to myself when I made a mistake?"
    - You can write answers down or just think about them for a few minutes.
3. **Mindful Check-Ins**
    - Taking one to two minutes to pause during the day and notice your thoughts or body sensations can be a mini form of reflection.
    - Ask yourself: "How am I feeling right now—physically and emotionally?"
    - This quick scan can prevent you from being on autopilot and helps you see small tensions or worries before they escalate.
4. **Meditation and Quiet Time**
    - Sitting silently, focusing on your breath, and allowing thoughts to come and go can create space for reflective insights.
    - Meditation is not about clearing your mind completely; it is about observing thoughts without attachment.
    - As you notice certain thoughts repeat, you gain clues about unresolved issues or hidden desires.
5. **Conversation with a Supportive Person**
    - Sometimes, reflecting out loud with a friend, counselor, or mentor can help you see your own mind more clearly.

- Hearing yourself explain a situation can reveal angles you might miss when you are alone.
- Make sure you choose someone who listens without judgment and does not rush to “fix” your feelings.

Overcoming Blocks to Self-Reflection

1. **Fear of Uncomfortable Truths**
    - Looking inside can stir up old pain or regrets. You might fear that if you dig too deep, you will find something you cannot handle.
    - **Tip**: Remind yourself that discovering pain is the first step to healing. You can always seek professional help if certain memories are too intense.
2. **Lack of Time or Energy**
    - In a busy life, setting aside quiet moments may feel impossible.
    - **Tip**: Schedule small windows—like 5 minutes before bed—to jot down a few thoughts. Even brief reflection can yield important insights.
3. **Worry About Self-Judgment**
    - If you have a history of being very hard on yourself, you might avoid reflecting for fear of criticism.
    - **Tip**: Set a rule that you will notice your thoughts and feelings, but will not label them as good or bad. Approach yourself as if you were a kind observer.
4. **Impatience for Quick Results**
    - Self-reflection is a gradual process. You might want instant clarity, but that is rarely how it works.
    - **Tip**: Think of reflection as a daily or weekly practice, not a one-time event. Insights build up bit by bit.
5. **Comparing Yourself to Others**
    - You may think, “Other people do not spend this much time on inner work,” or “I should be normal and not think about this stuff.”
    - **Tip**: Everyone’s path is unique. Reflecting on yourself is a sign of self-respect, not a sign of weakness.

How Self-Reflection Helps Your Inner Child

When you reflect on your triggers and responses, you might discover that certain reactions date back to childhood experiences. For example, feeling panicked when someone raises their voice because it reminds you of harsh scolding in early life. By identifying these roots, you can comfort that younger side of you instead of getting stuck in fear or anger. In essence, self-reflection opens a channel of communication between your adult self and the child who once felt ignored or misunderstood.

Practical Exercises for Self-Reflection

Exercise 1: The "Why" Ladder

1. Think about a recent situation that upset you—maybe you felt sudden rage or sadness.
2. Ask yourself "Why did I feel that way?" Write or think of the answer.
3. Then ask "Why?" again regarding that answer.
4. Repeat this step about five times. Each "why" digs a bit deeper into the core issue.
5. You might discover that your strong reaction ties to an early experience or a basic fear of being alone, unworthy, etc.

Exercise 2: Daily Emotional Notes

1. Keep a small notebook or use a phone app to log your main emotion at least three times a day—morning, midday, evening.
2. Write a sentence or two about any clear reason behind that emotion: "I am anxious because I have a presentation," or "I feel calm after a good talk with a friend."
3. Look back at your notes after a week. Are there patterns? Particular times of day or certain events that trigger certain feelings?

Exercise 3: Reflective Dialogue with Your Younger Self

1. Set aside a quiet moment.
2. Imagine your younger self is sitting in front of you.
3. Ask them how they feel and what they want you to know.
4. Write down any impressions, words, or images that come up, even if they seem random.
5. See if these impressions shed light on your current behaviors or emotional wounds.

Common Mistakes in Self-Reflection

1. **Overfocusing on Negatives**
    - It is easy to get wrapped up in everything that is wrong. This might lead you to miss positive changes or strengths.
    - **Solution**: Remember to notice progress, no matter how small, and celebrate little wins.
2. **Believing All Thoughts Are Accurate**
    - Not all thoughts reflect absolute truth. Sometimes, old beliefs or fears distort reality.
    - **Solution**: When a thought pops up, ask if it is fact-based or if it might be colored by past experiences or anxieties.
3. **Holding onto Self-Blame**
    - If you find you made an error, you might turn that into a global statement like, "I am just terrible at everything."
    - **Solution**: Resist absolute phrases like "always" or "never." Keep perspective: a mistake in one area does not define you as a whole person.
4. **Refusing to Adjust**
    - You might uncover the root cause of a certain reaction but do not take any steps to respond differently next time.
    - **Solution**: Reflection is a tool for change. After you gain insight, decide on a small action to do differently.
5. **Comparing Timelines**
    - Reflecting on your inner world can lead you to think you should have solved all your issues by now.

    - **Solution**: Healing is not a race. Each individual moves at their own pace, and it is natural to discover deeper layers over time.

Real-Life Examples of Self-Reflection

1. **Case: Joel and Work Stress**
    - **Situation**: Joel noticed he felt extremely anxious every time his boss asked for a progress report.
    - **Reflection**: By journaling, he realized that as a child, his father would become furious whenever Joel brought home less-than-perfect grades. This left him believing that any request for an update was a setup for criticism.
    - **Outcome**: Understanding this, Joel began reminding himself that his boss was not his father and that asking for a progress report was a standard part of the job. Over weeks of reflection, he grew calmer and even started to speak openly with his boss about any concerns.
2. **Case: Rosa and Social Gatherings**
    - **Situation**: Rosa found herself declining most invitations, even though she felt lonely. She did not understand her own hesitation.
    - **Reflection**: Through guided questions in a journal, she discovered that she feared people would find her boring or weird, a fear rooted in repeated bullying in middle school.
    - **Outcome**: Realizing this was an old wound, she told herself that not everyone is like the bullies from her past. She then set a goal to accept at least one invite a month. Over time, she found supportive friends who liked her as she was.
3. **Case: Amir and Financial Anxiety**
    - **Situation**: Amir became extremely stressed about money, checking his bank account every hour.
    - **Reflection**: By using a mindful check-in practice, Amir discovered that his fear of being broke traced back to childhood, when his family sometimes struggled to pay bills. He unconsciously felt that any dip in his account balance threatened his basic security.
    - **Outcome**: He began writing affirmations reminding himself that he had a stable job and was making responsible choices. This reduced

the panic around finances and let him enjoy his earnings in a balanced way.

Lesser-Known Tips for Effective Self-Reflection

1. **Use Imagery**
   - Sometimes visualizing your thoughts as objects can help. For example, if you see your fear as a heavy box you are carrying, you can imagine setting it down. This symbolic act can ease your emotional load.
2. **Change Locations**
   - Try reflecting in different places—a park bench, a corner of your living room, or even inside your car (parked, of course). Sometimes a shift in environment unlocks new insights.
3. **Set Up Rituals**
   - Small rituals, like lighting a candle or sipping tea, can signal to your brain that it is time for reflection. This can help you feel safer and more focused.
4. **Involve Physical Movement**
   - If sitting still feels stifling, walk slowly while you reflect. Notice your surroundings, your breathing, and the thoughts that arise. This blend of movement and thought can loosen mental blocks.
5. **Record Audio Notes**
   - If writing is not your style, use a phone's voice recorder to speak your reflections. Hearing your own voice can reveal emotional nuances you might miss in silent thinking.

Handling Strong Emotions During Reflection

Self-reflection can uncover intense feelings like shame, rage, or deep sadness. Here's how to cope:

1. **Pause and Breathe**
   - If you feel overwhelmed, step back and take slow, even breaths for a minute or two.
   - Acknowledge the feeling without forcing it away.

2. **Seek Comfort**
    - If you can, have a favorite blanket, calming music, or a warm drink on hand. Self-soothing helps contain strong emotions.
3. **Talk to Someone**
    - If reflection brings up severe distress, reach out to a friend, counselor, or support line. You do not have to face everything alone.
4. **Return Later**
    - It is okay to take breaks. You can come back to the reflection when you feel more grounded.
5. **Short Visualizations**
    - If you recall a scary memory, briefly imagine giving your younger self a supportive hug. Reassure them that things are different now, and you have more control.

How to Integrate Self-Reflection into Daily Life

1. **Morning Check**
    - Upon waking, spend a minute noticing how you feel. Are you tired, eager, anxious? A quick note in a journal or a mental acknowledgment can set the tone.
2. **Lunch Pause**
    - Midday, do a brief reflection on how the first part of your day went. Any surprises? Any emotional spikes? Make a mental or written note.
3. **Evening Wrap-Up**
    - Before bed, jot down key events of the day. Note emotions, thoughts, or lessons learned. Doing this prevents you from carrying unresolved feelings to sleep.
4. **Weekly Review**
    - Once a week, look over your journal or mental notes. See if any patterns jump out—like repeated frustration in certain contexts, or improvements in handling stress.
5. **Monthly or Quarterly Deep Reflection**
    - Set aside a longer session every month or every three months for in-depth reflection. You can revisit major personal themes, refine goals, and note progress in emotional healing.

Realistic Expectations for Self-Reflection

- **It Takes Time**: Consistent, gentle efforts bring lasting benefits, while expecting one "big breakthrough" can lead to disappointment.
- **It's Personal**: A method that works wonders for a friend may not feel right to you. Explore various approaches.
- **It Can Be Both Uplifting and Unsettling**: Discovering positives in yourself can be joyful, but confronting painful memories might be tough. Both sides are part of growth.
- **Support Is Valuable**: You do not have to do all reflection alone. A counselor, a trusted friend, or a support group can guide you if you get stuck.

How Self-Reflection Links to Other Skills in This Book

- **Trusting Your Own Thoughts (Chapter 5)**: Reflecting regularly helps confirm whether your thoughts make sense or stem from old fears. It strengthens the practice of self-trust.
- **Breaking Harmful Patterns (Chapter 6)**: Identifying these patterns is easier when you reflect consistently on triggers and reactions.
- **Handling Shame and Guilt (Chapter 8)**: Self-reflection can reveal where shame originated. It also helps separate current reality from past beliefs.
- **Setting Clear Goals (Chapter 16)**: Reflection clarifies what truly matters, guiding you to form goals aligned with your authentic needs.

Practical Tips to Keep Going

- **Don't Force It**: If you feel blocked, try a different reflection method. For instance, switch from journaling to a few minutes of silent thought, or talk to a friend.
- **Balance Private Reflection and Outside Input**: Sometimes hearing an external viewpoint can spark fresh insights. Use both personal time and shared conversations.

- **Acknowledge Changes**: Even if small, noticing a shift—like reacting less intensely to a trigger—encourages you to continue.
- **Set Boundaries for Rumination**: If you start going in circles, set a timer. When it rings, shift to a different activity or focus. Reflection should help, not trap you in negativity.

Conclusion of Chapter 15

Practicing self-reflection is a cornerstone of emotional growth and inner child healing. By looking honestly at your internal experiences—feelings, thoughts, memories—you create room for awareness and transformation. You learn what drives your actions, which beliefs might be outdated, and how childhood wounds still echo in your adult life. These insights can guide healthier choices, stronger relationships, and a gentler view of yourself.

Though it can be uncomfortable at first, especially if you have rarely paused to look within, self-reflection is worth the effort. It is a skill you can refine with brief daily check-ins, journaling, or mindful conversation. Over time, you will likely see that knowing yourself more deeply leads to self-compassion and better emotional management. In the next chapter, we will build on this by learning to set clear goals, another key step in steering your life in a direction that genuinely fits your evolving self.

CHAPTER 16: SETTING CLEAR GOALS

Introduction

Once you have spent time learning about your inner child, handling shame, and practicing self-reflection, you might wonder how to move forward in a structured way. This is where goal-setting comes in. Goals give direction to your healing and personal growth. They help you break down aspirations into concrete steps and track progress. Whether you want to improve relationships, overcome specific fears, or strengthen boundaries, creating clear goals guides your day-to-day actions and keeps you motivated.

In this chapter, we will explore why goal-setting is vital for emotional well-being, how to choose goals that suit your personal journey, and tips for avoiding common pitfalls like perfectionism or burnout. We will also look at how to link your goals to inner child healing, making sure your objectives align with the deeper changes you want in your life.

Why Goals Matter in Emotional Healing

1. **Give Structure to Growth**
   Goals turn vague wishes into action steps. Instead of saying, "I want to feel less anxious," you create a plan—like practicing a breathing exercise each morning. This provides clarity and a sense of purpose.
2. **Provide Motivation**
   Having a target can boost your energy. Each milestone you reach confirms that change is possible, encouraging you to keep going.
3. **Prevent Overwhelm**
   When your mind is full of unresolved wounds or many things you want to improve, goals help you focus on one area at a time. This reduces stress and helps you avoid feeling lost.
4. **Measure Progress**
   Emotional growth can be subtle, making it hard to see changes. Goals give you specific markers—like feeling calmer in social settings or stating your needs in a relationship—that you can observe over time.

5. **Boost Self-Trust**
   Each time you set a goal and follow through, even partially, you prove to yourself that you can direct your own path. This affirms that your thoughts and decisions are meaningful.

The Difference Between Healthy and Harmful Goals

- **Healthy Goals**:
  - Specific enough to guide action.
  - Aligned with your real values, not driven by social pressure.
  - Realistic, considering your time, energy, and resources.
  - Flexible enough to adapt if circumstances change.
- **Harmful Goals**:
  - Extremely rigid or demanding.
  - Based on pleasing others rather than your own needs.
  - Unrealistic (e.g., wanting to fix decades of emotional wounds in two weeks).
  - Tied to your worth as a person (e.g., believing you are worthless if you do not reach the goal exactly).

Deciding What Goals to Pursue

1. **Reflect on Your Inner Child's Needs**
   - Think about what your younger self might have lacked—love, stability, expression, or confidence. Choose goals that address these gaps. For instance, if you lacked emotional support, you might set a goal to form closer friendships or find a counselor.
2. **Check Your Current Struggles**
   - Look at what causes you the most stress or pain now—anxiety in social situations, poor boundaries, or self-doubt. Frame goals that aim to reduce these pressures.
3. **Prioritize**
   - If you have a long list, pick the one or two items that feel most urgent or foundational. Overloading yourself with too many goals at once can lead to burnout.

4. **Balance Long-Term and Short-Term**
    - A short-term goal might be to spend five minutes each morning in calm reflection. A long-term goal might be building a stable career path or improving family communication. Both matter, but start with tasks you can do in the near future.
5. **Listen to Your Feelings**
    - If you notice excitement or relief when you think about a goal, it might be a good fit. If you feel dread or shame, ask yourself if the goal is truly yours or if it comes from someone else's expectations.

How to Make Goals Manageable: The SMART Approach

Many people use the SMART format to ensure goals are practical:

1. **Specific**: Define the goal clearly. Instead of "I want to be healthy," say, "I will walk for 20 minutes three times a week."
2. **Measurable**: Have a way to track progress. Number of minutes walked, times you practiced a skill, etc.
3. **Achievable**: Make it challenging yet doable given your current reality. If you have never done exercise, promising daily one-hour runs might be too steep a jump.
4. **Relevant**: The goal should tie into your bigger emotional or personal needs. Is it helping your healing, confidence, or mental clarity?
5. **Time-Bound**: Set a timeframe, even if it is just a weekly check. This prevents open-ended intentions that never move forward.

Linking Goals to Inner Child Healing

1. **Include Comfort and Nurture**
    - If your younger self felt neglected, a goal could be: "Once a week, do something calming just for myself—like a warm bath, creative project, or relaxing walk."
2. **Address Old Fears**
    - If your child side was often scared, a goal might be: "Practice a gentle grounding technique whenever I feel panic rise."
3. **Build Self-Expression**

    - If you were silenced as a child, set a goal to speak your opinion in safe settings at least once a day, or write them down if verbal expression feels too risky at first.
4. **Celebrate Small Wins**
    - The child in you may have rarely received praise. Make sure to note each step you achieve. This does not have to be public fanfare—just a quiet acknowledgment that you did something good for yourself.
5. **Involve Positive Role Models**
    - If you lacked supportive adults, a goal might be to find a mentor or join a supportive group. Observing healthy behaviors can heal old beliefs about being alone.

Potential Obstacles in Goal-Setting

1. **Perfectionism**
    - You might feel if you cannot do it perfectly, you should not do it at all.
    - **Tip**: Emphasize progress, not perfection. Even partial completion of a goal is better than quitting.
2. **Procrastination**
    - Fear of failure can lead to putting tasks off.
    - **Tip**: Break down goals into tiny steps. For example, "Write for 5 minutes today," not "Finish a whole chapter."
3. **Setting Goals for Others**
    - If your goal is about changing someone else, it may lead to frustration since you cannot control them.
    - **Tip**: Focus on what you can do or how you can respond. For instance, instead of "Make my partner be more affectionate," aim for "Communicate my needs clearly and calmly."
4. **Comparing to Others' Goals**
    - You might set goals because you see friends doing them, even if it does not fit your life.
    - **Tip**: Remember your own path and needs. Goals must come from your own heart, not peer pressure.
5. **Lack of Support**

    - Without moral support or accountability, it can be tough to follow through.
    - **Tip**: If possible, share your goal with a friend or group, or keep a progress journal. Sometimes just writing it down makes it feel more real.

Steps to Create a Goal Plan

1. **Brainstorm**
    - List all the changes or improvements you want. Do not hold back. Then narrow down the list.
2. **Pick One Main Goal**
    - Choose the one you feel is most pressing or that would have the biggest positive effect on your life right now.
3. **Break It Into Mini-Goals**
    - For instance, if your main goal is to build confidence in social settings, mini-goals might be:
        - Practice a short greeting to a new coworker once a week.
        - Speak up in a small meeting at least once.
        - Attend a social event for 30 minutes, then allow yourself to leave if you feel overwhelmed.
4. **Decide on Measurements**
    - How will you know you are succeeding? For social goals, it might be counting how many times you speak up in a week. For stress management, it might be logging daily relaxation exercises.
5. **Set a Timeframe**
    - Give yourself a reasonable period—like a month or six weeks—to work on these steps. You can review and adjust as needed.
6. **Plan for Obstacles**
    - Think about potential hurdles, like feeling too shy on certain days or having a busy schedule. Brainstorm ways around them, such as scheduling tasks on less hectic days.
7. **Reevaluate**
    - After the set time, examine what happened. Did you meet the goals? If not, do you need more time, or a new approach?

Balancing Goals with Self-Care

When working on goals, there is a risk of becoming overly strict with yourself. Remember that you have emotional needs that might not fit a rigid plan. Some days, stress or memories might sap your energy.

- **Allow Flexibility**: If you miss a step, do not treat it as total failure. Adjust and keep going.
- **Self-Kindness**: Remind yourself that progress is rarely in a straight line. Inner child healing can involve setbacks, tears, or needing rest.
- **Rest Days**: Build in days when you do not push forward on goals, especially if you are feeling emotionally raw.
- **Celebrate**: Each small achievement deserves a moment of acknowledgment—just a mental note that you moved forward.

Real-Life Goal-Setting Examples

1. **Case: Priya's Self-Worth Goal**
    - **Situation**: Priya realized her sense of self-worth depended on external praise.
    - **Goal**: Write down one personal strength each day, without waiting for anyone else to confirm it.
    - **Mini-Steps**:
        - Keep a small notebook by the bed.
        - Each morning, note a quality or skill she appreciates about herself (e.g., kindness to a neighbor, finishing a task at work).
    - **Outcome**: After a month, Priya noticed she felt more confident, even if no one gave her compliments.
2. **Case: Luis's Anger Management Goal**
    - **Situation**: Luis wanted to reduce angry outbursts at home.
    - **Goal**: Practice a one-minute breathing exercise before responding whenever he felt anger flaring.
    - **Mini-Steps**:
        - Place a reminder note in the kitchen: "Pause and breathe."
        - Log each instance he successfully paused before speaking.

    - **Outcome**: Over a few weeks, he managed to cut down on harsh words by nearly half. He still felt anger but channeled it more constructively.
3. **Case: Hana's Social Comfort Goal**
    - **Situation**: Hana felt extreme anxiety in group gatherings.
    - **Goal**: Increase comfort level at social events by attending at least one small event a month and staying for at least 20 minutes.
    - **Mini-Steps**:
        - Start with a friend's casual get-together instead of a large party.
        - Use calming self-talk beforehand ("It's okay to be nervous, but I can handle this.")
        - Leave after 20 minutes if truly uncomfortable, or stay longer if feeling alright.
    - **Outcome**: After three months, Hana noticed that her anxiety lessened each time, and she even stayed an hour at one gathering.

Practical Exercises for Goal-Setting

Exercise 1: The Value Check

1. Write down what matters most to you right now: family, creativity, financial security, peace of mind, etc.
2. Pick one or two values you feel you have neglected.
3. Form a goal that connects to those values. For instance, if you neglected creativity, maybe your goal is to spend 30 minutes a week painting or writing.

Exercise 2: Obstacle Brainstorm

1. Choose a goal you want.
2. List every possible obstacle you can think of, no matter how small.
3. For each obstacle, write one possible solution.
4. This prepares you mentally and makes the goal more realistic.

Exercise 3: Visualizing Success

1. Sit comfortably and close your eyes.
2. Picture yourself having completed the goal. What does your life look like? How do you feel?
3. Notice details—like who is around you, how your body feels, what you are doing differently.
4. Keep this image in mind when you feel doubt, using it as motivation.

Lesser-Known Tips for Making Goals Stick (Extra Useful Insights)

1. **Create a Support Board**
    - Place sticky notes with your goals somewhere visible—like a wall or a fridge. Each time you complete a step, move the note to a "done" section. This gives a visual sense of progress.
2. **Plan Rewards**
    - A small reward (like a relaxing bath, a favorite snack, or a new book) each time you hit a milestone can boost morale. Make sure it is something healthy that genuinely brings you joy.
3. **Adjust Language**
    - Instead of "I have to do this," phrase it as "I choose to do this to help myself." This shift supports a sense of empowerment rather than obligation.
4. **Short Accountability Messages**
    - If you have a friend or relative who respects your efforts, send them quick updates. For example, "I practiced my relaxation routine today," or "I managed to speak up once in class." They do not have to give feedback; just telling someone can reinforce success.
5. **Focus on Feelings as Well as Action**
    - Sometimes your goal might be about a state of mind, like "I want to feel more relaxed in the evening." Then you list actions that might produce that feeling, such as turning off electronics an hour before bed or reading a calm book. This merges tangible steps with emotional aims.

Checking In on Your Goals

- **Regular Reviews**: Every week or two, ask yourself how well you are following through. Are you consistent with the steps you outlined?
- **Revision is Okay**: If a goal feels too big or too small, change it. It is not failure; it is adapting to reality.
- **Celebrate Partial Success**: If you aimed to do something five times and only managed three times, that is still progress. Recognizing partial wins keeps you motivated.

Potential Emotional Reactions to Goal-Setting

- **Excitement**: The idea of moving forward can be thrilling, fueling determination.
- **Anxiety**: Fear of failing or fear of succeeding (and then facing new challenges) can surface.
- **Doubt**: You may question if you can really change or if you deserve improvement.
- **Hope**: Seeing even small changes can spark optimism, especially if you have felt stuck for a long time.

How Goals Support Inner Child Healing

Each goal you set that nurtures safety, expression, or self-care corrects old messages that you did not matter. Achieving even small milestones sends a signal to the younger you that your needs are important enough to plan for. Over time, this consistent care shifts the deeper narrative from one of neglect or fear to one of self-guided growth and compassion.

How This Links to Reflection (Chapter 15) and Beyond

- **Reflection Guides Goal Choices**: By looking at your patterns and needs, you discover what goals align with your deeper self.

- **Goals Inspire Further Reflection**: As you work on a goal, new insights come up—like hidden resistances or unexpected joys. You reflect on these findings to refine your path.
- **Supports Other Areas of Healing**: Setting goals around boundaries, self-kindness, or trust helps cement the lessons from earlier chapters in daily life.

Conclusion of Chapter 16

Setting clear goals gives shape to your healing journey and personal growth. By breaking big aspirations into smaller tasks, you create a pathway that you can follow step by step. Goals keep you focused, help you track progress, and motivate you to stay the course when challenges arise. When chosen wisely—aligned with your real needs, manageable in scope, and grounded in self-compassion—they can transform vague dreams into achievable realities.

As you design your goals, remember to connect them to the deeper emotional changes you want, including the care your inner child never received. By doing so, you ensure your outer actions match your inner healing. In the following chapters, we will expand on skills like self-coaching and developing helpful routines that further support these goals. As you proceed, keep celebrating each bit of progress, no matter how small. Each step forward is a gift to your adult self and the child within.

CHAPTER 17: SELF-COACHING SKILLS

Introduction

Self-coaching skills are methods you use to guide your own actions, thoughts, and emotional states without needing someone else to lead you. While professional coaches or counselors can offer valuable insight, we often spend a lot of time on our own—facing daily tasks, decisions, and emotional ups and downs by ourselves. Having self-coaching skills gives you the power to address challenges as they come, rather than waiting for the next therapy session or friend's advice.

In this chapter, we will explore what self-coaching skills are, why they matter for anyone healing their inner child, and how to develop them in practical ways. We will also discuss common barriers, such as negative self-talk or uncertainty, and how to overcome these. By the end of this chapter, you should have a clearer understanding of how to be your own guide as you move through everyday life.

Why Self-Coaching Skills Matter

1. **Boosts Independence**
   You cannot always rely on external support. Self-coaching lets you handle many day-to-day emotions and decisions on your own. This does not mean you never seek help—it simply gives you a stronger base.
2. **Encourages Ongoing Growth**
   When you can coach yourself, you maintain momentum between counseling sessions or life events. You do not have to pause your emotional growth because no one is available to talk.
3. **Aligns with Inner Child Healing**
   Developing a kinder, more guiding inner voice helps the child side of you feel safer. Instead of harsh self-criticism, you learn to offer yourself calm direction, as a good mentor or teacher would.
4. **Builds Resourcefulness**
   Self-coaching can help you find solutions under stress, identify your strengths, and see options you might otherwise miss. It prompts you to ask, "How can I help myself here?"

5. **Fosters Lasting Habits**
   Many changes require consistent effort: managing anxiety, building confidence, or learning boundaries. Self-coaching sets up routines and reminders so you keep going, even when motivation dips.

What Is Self-Coaching?

Self-coaching is the act of talking yourself through problems, encouraging yourself during low moods, and planning strategies to reach goals. It includes:

- **Self-Observation**: Watching your own behaviors and responses—much like a coach studies an athlete's performance.
- **Inquiry and Curiosity**: Asking questions that challenge negative assumptions or expand your thinking.
- **Practical Tools**: Using techniques, checklists, or exercises to steady your emotions, brainstorm solutions, or track improvements.
- **Kind Accountability**: Holding yourself responsible for your actions, but in a gentle, supportive tone.

Common Barriers to Good Self-Coaching

1. **Harsh Inner Voice**
   - If you grew up hearing criticism or blame, you might have absorbed that into your own mental dialogue.
   - **Result**: Instead of coaching yourself with compassion, you might berate yourself for mistakes.
2. **Doubting Your Abilities**
   - You may think, "I can't guide myself. I need someone wiser."
   - **Result**: You do not try self-coaching at all, missing out on a tool that can strengthen your independence.
3. **Confusion About Tools**
   - Some people do not know which techniques or exercises to use, so they give up quickly.
   - **Result**: Self-coaching attempts feel random and unhelpful without a structure.
4. **Fear of Taking Responsibility**

    - Guiding yourself means admitting you have control over some parts of life, which can be scary if you have been used to a sense of helplessness.
    - **Result**: You might avoid self-coaching because it forces you to face your own power.
5. **Irregular Practice**
    - Like any skill, self-coaching requires steady application. Using it once and stopping will not yield real change.
    - **Result**: Sporadic use prevents you from forming the habit and benefiting fully.

Shifting from Self-Criticism to Self-Coaching

A critical inner voice says things like, "You always fail," or "You should be ashamed." A coaching inner voice is more like, "Yes, this is tough, but let's think of a way to handle it."

Steps to Move Toward a Coaching Mindset

1. **Notice the Tone**
    - Pay attention when you talk to yourself. Is it harsh or supportive?
2. **Replace Criticism with Questions**
    - Instead of "I messed up again," try, "How can I learn from this?" or "What's the next small step?"
3. **Acknowledge Difficulty**
    - A good coach recognizes challenges. "This is hard, but I can break it down."
4. **Offer Understanding, Not Excuses**
    - You can recognize where you went wrong without attacking your worth. "I see why I acted that way, but I want to choose differently next time."

Building Self-Coaching Skills Step by Step

1. **Start with Awareness**
    - Watch your actions and moods for a few days. Write short notes on situations where you felt lost or upset. Ask yourself, "What was going on, and how did I talk to myself about it?"

    - This creates a baseline understanding of how you handle stress or confusion without external guidance.
2. **Pick a Simple Tool**
    - Choose one method for self-coaching to begin with. For example, a short question list, a breathing exercise, or a quick pep talk.
    - Each time you face a challenge, pause to use this tool.
3. **Apply the Tool Consistently**
    - For at least a week, try using the same method whenever a small problem arises—like feeling rushed, irritated, or uncertain.
    - This repetition builds comfort with the process of self-coaching.
4. **Evaluate and Adjust**
    - After using a tool for a while, reflect. Did it help you calm down or find a solution? If not, tweak it or try another technique.
    - The point is to shape a set of methods that fit your unique thinking style.
5. **Expand Your Toolkit**
    - Over time, gather multiple exercises—like question prompts, quick journaling, short meditations, or mindful check-ins.
    - Different situations might require different approaches. Having several options prevents you from feeling stuck.

Useful Self-Coaching Methods

1. **Guided Questions**
    - Prepare a small list of questions to ask yourself when stressed or confused. Examples:
        - "What's really bothering me right now?"
        - "Is there a small step I can take to feel better?"
        - "What do I need—rest, information, or help from someone?"
2. **The "Reset" Pause**
    - When you catch yourself in negative self-talk, say (in your mind or quietly out loud), "Stop."
    - Take three slow, deep breaths.
    - Ask, "What is the truth of this situation, not just my fear?"
    - This brief pause can shift you from reacting to guiding yourself.
3. **Role-Play a Supportive Mentor**
    - Imagine you are a wise, kind mentor speaking to your younger self.

    - Describe the problem, then give calm advice, as you would to a close friend.
    - Note any insights that come from this shift in perspective.
4. **Positive Evidence Collection**
    - When you doubt you can solve something, list times you handled similar issues well in the past.
    - This helps combat the idea that you "always fail" and reminds you of actual successes.
5. **Obstacle-and-Solution Brainstorm**
    - If you face a big hurdle, write down every possible barrier you see.
    - Next to each barrier, list at least one solution, even if small.
    - This approach transforms the problem from an overwhelming wall into a set of smaller, solvable tasks.

Linking Self-Coaching to Inner Child Healing

- **Offering the Guidance You Missed**: If the child side of you never received calm, supportive direction, self-coaching fills that gap by speaking to yourself in a nurturing tone.
- **Rewriting Past Patterns**: Old habits might say, "You are helpless" or "You cannot fix anything." Self-coaching replaces these lines with, "You can figure out a next step."
- **Undoing Dependency**: If you relied on others to solve problems because your childhood taught you that you had no power, self-coaching reintroduces the idea that you are capable.
- **Consistent Encouragement**: That younger side needs ongoing reassurance. Regular self-coaching sessions act like mini pep talks, letting the child inside know that someone (you) has their back.

Overcoming Resistance to Self-Coaching

1. **"I Don't Deserve Kindness"**
    - Some people feel they must be tough on themselves to avoid laziness or self-pity. However, harshness often leads to anxiety and more mistakes.

    - **Alternative**: Try a more balanced approach. Recognize that mistakes happen, and ask how to address them constructively.
2. **"It's Too Awkward"**
    - Talking to yourself or writing notes might feel strange at first. That is normal. Many new habits feel odd before they become second nature.
    - **Alternative**: Start with brief mental coaching: "I can handle this step." If writing or speaking out loud is too uncomfortable, think your way through the guidance quietly.
3. **"I Need an Expert, Not Just Myself"**
    - Professional help is valuable, but you do not see your counselor 24/7. Between sessions or advice, you still need daily coping.
    - **Alternative**: Combine both. Use professional sessions to gain insights, then apply them through self-coaching techniques.
4. **"I Forget to Use These Skills When Stressed"**
    - In tough moments, it is easy to default to old reactions.
    - **Alternative**: Set reminders on your phone, place sticky notes around your home, or ask a friend to text you daily check-ins. Gradually, you will remember on your own.
5. **"I Worry I'll Make Things Worse"**
    - Self-coaching is about gentle solutions, not harsh commands. Unless you are ignoring major problems or denying reality, you are unlikely to harm yourself by exploring healthy self-guidance.
    - **Alternative**: Keep your approaches small and realistic, and if you find yourself in a crisis, reach out for professional or external help.

Real-Life Examples of Self-Coaching

1. **Case: Marco's Morning Anxiety**
    - **Situation**: Each morning, Marco woke up feeling overwhelmed by tasks. His mind raced with worries about work, finances, and personal errands.
    - **Self-Coaching Method**: He created a short question list by his bed:
        1. "What is the most important task today?"
        2. "What is one small step to start it?"
        3. "What can wait until later?"

    - **Outcome**: By going through these questions before getting up, Marco felt more focused. His anxiety lessened because he had a simple plan for the day.
2. **Case: Felicia's Negative Self-Talk**
    - **Situation**: Felicia often told herself she was not smart enough when she encountered challenging problems at work.
    - **Self-Coaching Method**: She decided to catch this negative voice and respond with a kinder approach: "Yes, this is hard, but I've solved tough issues before. Let me break it down."
    - **Outcome**: Over time, her self-doubt decreased. She did not become arrogant, but she found a balanced perspective that let her tackle problems without immediate defeatism.
3. **Case: Donovan's Social Fear**
    - **Situation**: Donovan struggled to speak up in group settings. He dreaded making a mistake or looking foolish.
    - **Self-Coaching Method**: He practiced a short script: "I might be nervous, but I can say one comment to add to the discussion. If it doesn't go well, I can learn from it and try again."
    - **Outcome**: This mental coaching gave him permission to be less than perfect. Eventually, Donovan spoke more freely, realizing people appreciated his contributions.

Practical Exercises to Strengthen Self-Coaching

Exercise 1: Three-Part Check-In

1. **Emotion**: Ask, "What am I feeling right now—anxiety, boredom, sadness?"
2. **Thought**: Ask, "Which thought is fueling that emotion?" (e.g., "I'm not good enough.")
3. **Next Step**: Ask, "What is one small action or new thought to try?" (e.g., "I will test this assumption by actually trying the task. I might be fine.")

Do this once a day or whenever you face a stumbling block.

Exercise 2: Written Self-Dialogue

1. Take a pen and paper (or a digital note).
2. Label one side "Me (Worried Part)" and another side "Me (Coach Part)."
3. Write one or two lines from the worried side (for example, "I'm scared I'll fail at this new responsibility").
4. Then write a response from the coach side (for example, "It's normal to feel scared. Let's plan the first step to start.").
5. Go back and forth for a page or two. Notice if your coach side grows more confident over time.

Exercise 3: Tiny Goal with Rewards

1. Choose a small, manageable goal—like tidying a corner of your room or reading for 10 minutes about a topic you find important.
2. Coach yourself by planning exactly when you will do it and how. ("On Tuesday evening, I will spend 15 minutes on it.")
3. When it is time, talk to yourself kindly as if you had a real-life coach: "I know you feel a bit tired, but we only need 15 minutes. Let's begin."
4. After completing the mini-goal, allow yourself a small positive reward or rest. Reflect on the fact that you guided yourself to completion.

Lesser-Known Insights for Self-Coaching (Extra Useful Tips)

1. **Use a "Confidence File"**
    - Keep a digital or physical folder of positive feedback—emails, texts, notes from friends praising your work or kindness. When self-doubt arises, look at this file to remind yourself of your strengths.
2. **Experiment with Voice Memos**
    - If writing feels slow, record voice memos to yourself. Replaying them can highlight patterns in your thinking and help you refine your coaching style.
3. **Body Movement**
    - Sometimes your mind is stuck, but moving your body can shift your internal state. Walk while you talk yourself through a

problem. You might find solutions come easier with physical motion.

4. **Link to an Existing Habit**
   - Pair self-coaching with a daily habit. For instance, while brushing your teeth or waiting for your morning coffee to brew, ask, "What do I want to focus on today?" or "What's one supportive thing I can tell myself right now?"
5. **Create a Personal Motto**
   - Make a short motto that captures your self-coaching spirit: "I learn as I go," "Step by step, I improve," or any phrase that feels motivating. Repeat it during tough moments to anchor your mindset.

Monitoring Progress in Self-Coaching

1. **Jot Down Successes**
   - Each day or week, list one moment where you coached yourself well. This acts as proof that you can do it again.
2. **Identify Stumbles**
   - If you reverted to harsh self-criticism, note the circumstances. Was it triggered by fatigue, a certain person, or an unexpected problem? Recognizing patterns helps you prepare next time.
3. **Adjust Your Methods**
   - If a question prompt or exercise stops being helpful, modify it. Self-coaching is about flexibility.
4. **Seek Occasional Feedback**
   - Talk to a trusted friend or counselor about your self-coaching journey. They might notice additional strengths or offer new ideas.
5. **Celebrate Small Wins**
   - Give yourself positive recognition for each instance of calm guidance or improved response. This builds momentum.

Handling Setbacks in Self-Coaching

- **"I Tried, But I Still Felt Overwhelmed"**: Self-coaching does not magically remove all tough emotions. Its goal is to reduce intensity and guide you to solutions. If you still feel overwhelmed, it may be time to reach out for professional help or supportive friends.

- **"I Forgot Everything in the Heat of the Moment"**: Stress can freeze your mind. That is why practicing these skills in calmer times is essential. Gradually, they become automatic under pressure.
- **"I Coached Myself But Made a Wrong Choice"**: Mistakes are part of learning. A good coach helps you review what happened, learn the lesson, and try again.
- **"I Feel Silly Talking to Myself"**: Self-talk is normal, though we rarely admit it publicly. Over time, the awkwardness usually fades, and you become comfortable guiding yourself internally.

How Self-Coaching Supports the Inner Child Long-Term

By consistently providing helpful guidance and reassurance, you give your inner child a stable adult presence that might have been missing in early years. Each time you use a gentle internal voice—saying, "We can solve this," or "It's okay to be nervous, let's see what we can do"—you rewrite the child's experience of being alone with big fears. Over time, this fosters a sense of security and trust that was once lacking. The child part of you begins to rely on your adult self as a safe leader, reducing panic and self-sabotage.

Summary of Key Points in Chapter 17

- **Self-coaching** is the practice of guiding your own thoughts, emotions, and decisions with kindness and structure.
- **Benefits** include increased independence, ongoing progress between therapy sessions, deeper inner child healing, and more robust life skills.
- **Barriers** include harsh self-criticism, lack of trust in your abilities, or forgetting to use these skills under stress.
- **Methods** involve guided questions, resetting your thoughts, role-playing a mentor, collecting positive evidence, and brainstorming solutions.
- **Progress** can be monitored through daily logs, reflections, and gentle adjustments to your techniques.

- **Link to Inner Child**: Self-coaching allows you to offer the stability and support that might have been missing during childhood.

By building strong self-coaching habits, you equip yourself with an internal support system that remains available around the clock. In the next chapter, we will learn about helpful routines for healing—small daily or weekly practices that keep your emotional health steady. These routines can pair beautifully with self-coaching skills, ensuring your progress remains consistent even when life gets busy or stressful.

CHAPTER 18: HELPFUL ROUTINES FOR HEALING

Introduction

We all benefit from having predictable rhythms in our lives. Helpful routines can act like anchors, providing comfort and stability in times of stress. For anyone working on healing the inner child, these routines are especially vital. They reinforce self-care, reduce anxiety, and allow steady progress over time. They are not about strict schedules or perfection; rather, they involve practical methods of caring for your body, mind, and emotions each day or week.

In this chapter, we will explore the concept of helpful routines for emotional healing. We will look at why they matter, how to design them, and how to stay flexible as life changes. We will also discuss ways to overcome common obstacles, such as getting bored or discouraged, and how to ensure these routines truly support your inner child's well-being. By the end, you will have a variety of ideas for daily, weekly, and occasional routines you can implement to keep your healing on track.

Why Routines Matter for Healing

1. **Predictability Eases Anxiety**
   When you face unknowns, having a few consistent habits can give a sense of safety. You might not control every aspect of life, but you can rely on certain calming steps each day.
2. **Reduces Overthinking**
   Deciding every day what to do for self-care can feel exhausting. Setting a routine removes some decision pressure—you know what activity comes next.
3. **Sustains Long-Term Growth**
   Emotional changes often need time to become embedded. Routines ensure you do not forget key practices, like breathing exercises or journaling, even after you start feeling better.

4. **Empowers the Inner Child**
   A predictable schedule can calm that younger side of you, which might have felt unstable or neglected in the past. Following through on a routine shows your child self that you keep promises.
5. **Allows Gradual Adjustment**
   Routines can start small and evolve. You do not need a rigid blueprint from day one. A few simple habits can expand as your needs change.

Types of Helpful Routines

1. **Morning Routines**
   - Activities you do soon after waking. This might include a quick body stretch, writing down a goal for the day, or repeating an encouraging phrase.
   - Purpose: Start the day with clarity and lower morning stress.
2. **Evening Routines**
   - Practices that help you wind down before sleep. Examples include reading for 10 minutes, doing a short relaxation technique, or writing in a gratitude log.
   - Purpose: Signal your mind that it's time to rest, reducing nighttime worries.
3. **Self-Care Routines**
   - Scheduled actions like taking a relaxing bath on Sunday evenings, or a midweek block of time to engage in a hobby.
   - Purpose: Ensure you make space for self-nurturing rather than letting busy schedules push it aside.
4. **Emotional Check-Ins**
   - Brief moments—maybe at lunch or before bed—where you scan your feelings, note any tension in your body, and see if you need extra support.
   - Purpose: Prevent bottled-up emotions by addressing them regularly.
5. **Movement Routines**
   - Gentle stretches, short walks, or any simple exercise at set times.
   - Purpose: Physical motion helps release stress chemicals and can improve mood, aiding emotional healing.
6. **Digital Breaks**

- Planned intervals where you step away from screens or social media.
- Purpose: Lower digital overload and create mental space for reflection or relaxation.

Designing a Routine That Fits You

1. **Identify Your Main Needs**
    - Do you need better rest, more fun, or less anxiety? Tailor your routine to solve your biggest challenges first.
2. **Start Small**
    - Aim for one or two habits to add to your day or week, like a short breathing exercise each morning and a 10-minute walk after lunch.
    - Overloading yourself at once can lead to frustration.
3. **Set Times or Triggers**
    - Link your new activity to a time (e.g., "right after breakfast") or a trigger (e.g., "when I feel tension in my shoulders"). This helps the routine become automatic.
4. **Make It Enjoyable**
    - If a habit feels like a boring chore, you are less likely to stick with it. Find methods that are pleasant or at least satisfying afterward, like a relaxing yoga stretch or a cozy reading nook.
5. **Write It Down**
    - Put your plan on paper or in your phone notes. The act of writing makes it more real. You can also check it occasionally to stay on track.

Possible Routines to Consider

1. **Morning Check-In with Inner Child**
    - Upon waking, spend a minute closing your eyes and picturing your younger self. Ask, "How are you feeling today?" If any worry or emotion surfaces, mentally respond with reassurance.
2. **Journaling Time**

    - Choose a set time—maybe before bed—to write down the day's highs and lows, your emotional state, or any insights. Consistent journaling builds self-awareness.
3. **Weekly Creative Hour**
    - One hour on a chosen day for a playful or creative activity (drawing, crafting, or simple music-making). Regular creativity relieves stress and nurtures the child side inside.
4. **Scheduled Breaks**
    - If you tend to work or think non-stop, plan two or three short breaks a day. Use these moments to breathe deeply, walk around, or just look out a window calmly.
5. **Physical Relaxation Routine**
    - End the day with 10 minutes of light stretching, focusing on tense muscles like the neck or shoulders. This can help release stored tension before sleep.
6. **Weekend Planning**
    - Dedicate part of your weekend to planning the upcoming week. Check your schedule, see where you can fit in self-care, and set priorities. This reduces anxiety about the unknown.

Overcoming Common Challenges

1. **Lack of Motivation**
    - In tough times, even simple tasks can feel heavy. Start with the easiest habit possible, like taking one slow, mindful breath each morning. Build from there.
2. **Boredom with Repetition**
    - Doing the same thing every day can get dull. Rotate between a few variations. For instance, if your nighttime routine is reading, vary the genre or medium (books vs. short articles).
3. **Fitting Routines into Busy Schedules**
    - If your days are packed, find micro-moments: a five-minute stretch when you wake, a short mindful pause at lunch, or a quick reflection while commuting (if it is safe to do so).
4. **Distractions and Interruptions**
    - Living with others or having an unpredictable job can disrupt your plan. Try to establish boundaries: let family know you need 15

minutes of quiet time, or pick times when you are least likely to be disturbed.

5. **Giving Up Too Soon**
    - Missing a day or two can make some people drop the routine entirely. Remember that slip-ups happen. Resume as soon as possible rather than labeling the effort a failure.

Routines to Aid Inner Child Comfort

1. **Small Daily Self-Affirmation**
    - Place a note on your mirror with words like, "You are worthy of care." Each morning or night, read it out loud to acknowledge yourself.
2. **Gentle Soothing Object**
    - If a comforting toy or soft blanket helps your inner child feel safe, keep it nearby during stressful times. Make it part of your wind-down routine.
3. **Visualizing a Safe Space**
    - Once or twice a day, close your eyes for a minute. Picture a place (real or imagined) where you felt or would feel protected. Stand or sit there mentally, breathing steadily, allowing that calm to sink in.
4. **Regular Check on Emotions**
    - Maybe at lunch, you ask yourself, "What is my main feeling right now?" If you sense fear or sadness, mentally reassure the younger side of you that you are present and listening.
5. **Playful Weekend Moments**
    - Reserve time each weekend for a fun activity you used to enjoy as a child—like drawing with crayons, building a simple craft, or doing a puzzle. This maintains a link to lightheartedness.

Real-Life Examples of Healing Routines

1. **Case: Jenny's "Quiet Tea Time"**
    - **Situation**: Jenny felt scattered after finishing work. She brought home stress and would snap at her partner.

  - **Routine**: She decided that upon arriving home, she would prepare a cup of tea, sit quietly for 10 minutes, and breathe. No phone, no TV.
  - **Outcome**: This became a soothing ritual that helped her switch from "work mode" to "home mode." Her partner noticed she was calmer. Jenny found that she decompressed more easily, and her evenings felt more pleasant.
2. **Case: Malcolm's "Sunday Sketch Hour"**
  - **Situation**: Malcolm realized he missed drawing, which he loved as a child. He also felt a lack of fun in his adult life.
  - **Routine**: Every Sunday afternoon, he set aside one hour to sketch anything—landscapes, doodles, or random shapes.
  - **Outcome**: At first, it felt odd to dedicate time to something that was not "productive." But the enjoyment and relaxation boosted his mood. He discovered that by Monday, he felt more inspired. This routine also reminded him that personal joy is important.
3. **Case: Selena's "Morning Mindful Stretch"**
  - **Situation**: Selena often woke up tense, worrying about the day ahead. Her back and shoulders ached.
  - **Routine**: She began a short set of stretches right after getting out of bed—focusing on shoulders, neck, and lower back. While stretching, she told herself, "I'm taking care of my body and mind."
  - **Outcome**: Her physical tension eased, and she started the day with a calmer mind. Over weeks, this routine became automatic, and she felt more energetic and grounded.

Practical Exercises for Building Routines

Exercise 1: Routine Brain Dump

1. Take a blank piece of paper or digital note.
2. Write down all possible self-care actions or tasks you wish to do regularly (stretching, journaling, quiet reading, short walks, etc.).
3. Circle one or two you feel most drawn to.
4. Decide a simple frequency—daily, twice a week, or weekly.
5. Commit to it for two weeks, then review if you want to keep it or modify it.

Exercise 2: Habit Pairing

1. Pick an existing habit you rarely skip—like brushing teeth, washing dishes, or preparing coffee in the morning.
2. Link a new healing action to it. For example, after you brush your teeth in the evening, you do a two-minute breathing exercise.
3. Keep the new action short and easy at first.
4. Over time, the older habit automatically triggers the new one, helping it stick.

Exercise 3: Weekly Reflection Slot

1. Choose a day of the week (perhaps Sunday evening).
2. Allocate 15–30 minutes for reflecting on how the past week went—emotions, wins, struggles.
3. Write down any small changes you want for the next week.
4. Over months, this weekly reflection helps you spot patterns in your progress and refine your routines.

Tips to Stay Flexible and Motivated

1. **Update Routines as You Grow**
   - What helped you last month may not be the same as you move forward. It is okay to swap activities or change the duration.
2. **Use Friendly Accountability**
   - If you have a friend who also wants to maintain routines, check in with each other. A quick text saying, "I did my morning stretch!" can reinforce your commitment.
3. **Set Reminders**
   - Phone alarms, calendar notifications, or even sticky notes can help you remember. Over time, you might not need them as the habit becomes ingrained.
4. **Reward Yourself Wisely**

    - Small treats or relaxing activities can serve as recognition for sticking to the routine. Pick rewards that truly make you feel content or recharged.
5. **Focus on Process, Not Perfection**
    - If you miss a day or feel the routine was not done "perfectly," avoid throwing it all away. Return to it as soon as you can.

Lesser-Known Methods to Refresh Your Routines

1. **Seasonal Adjustments**
    - Change certain practices based on the season. For instance, in warmer months, do more outdoor walks; in colder months, focus on indoor creative tasks or cozy reading. This prevents monotony.
2. **Mini Routines for Quick Emotional Resets**
    - Design a 5-minute emotional first-aid routine for moments of sudden stress. It could include a short breathing exercise, a kind phrase to yourself, and a glass of water.
3. **Use Visual Cues**
    - Put items you need for your routine in sight. For morning stretches, lay out your mat the night before. For journaling, keep your notebook on your pillow so you remember before sleep.
4. **Tie It to a Positive Feeling**
    - Remind yourself each time you do the routine why it matters: "This evening reading calms me," or "This journaling spot clears my mind." Linking it with the emotional benefit strengthens motivation.
5. **Include Random Fun**
    - Every so often, replace your usual routine with something playful—like dancing to a song instead of taking your typical short walk. Spontaneous changes keep things fresh.

Addressing Setbacks with Routines

- **"I Kept It Up for a While, Then Stopped Entirely"**: Life events (illness, travel, a big project) can disrupt habits. When ready, restart with a smaller version.

- **"It Feels Like a Chore Now"**: Try a different time of day, or swap in a new activity. Refreshing your approach can reignite interest.
- **"I Don't See Quick Results"**: Emotional or physical changes may be subtle. Log your mood or energy levels, so you can spot gradual improvements.
- **"Others in My Home Don't Respect My Routine"**: Gently communicate its importance or find pockets of time when you are less likely to be disturbed. If that is still not possible, adapt by doing partial routines or smaller actions until you can create more personal space.

Long-Term Benefits of Maintaining Helpful Routines

1. **Steady Emotional Baseline**
    - Consistent practices like journaling or relaxation lower overall stress and help you bounce back from setbacks more quickly.
2. **Reduced Feelings of Chaos**
    - Even if the outside world is unpredictable, these self-created habits ground you, offering a daily sense of accomplishment.
3. **Improved Sleep and Energy**
    - Evening routines, in particular, can enhance sleep quality, which in turn boosts mood and daily performance.
4. **Enhanced Self-Belief**
    - Following through on routines builds trust in your own reliability. This trust seeps into other areas, like decision-making and emotional resilience.
5. **Deepened Inner Child Healing**
    - Regular care signals to the younger you that you are now in charge, consistent, and caring. Over time, this can lessen fear or shame carried from the past.

Conclusion of Chapter 18

Helpful routines are like small, dependable steps you can take repeatedly to care for your mind, body, and inner child. They do not require major revamps or large blocks of time; even short, regular actions can shift your emotional landscape. By deciding which routines align with your greatest needs—be it better rest, creative expression, or daily calm—you lay out a supportive framework for healing.

The key is to keep routines flexible, enjoyable, and in tune with your current stage of growth. If you miss a day or find an activity stale, adjust without self-blame. Over time, these ongoing habits serve as a gentle, consistent reminder to protect your well-being. In the chapters ahead, we will explore personal growth strategies and long-term maintenance, building on the stable foundation these routines provide. For now, consider how you might begin (or refine) one simple daily or weekly routine that speaks to your heart and nurtures the child within.

CHAPTER 19: PERSONAL GROWTH STRATEGIES

Introduction

Personal growth involves learning new ideas and behaviors that help you handle life's challenges in a healthier way. It is not about becoming a perfect person. Instead, it means recognizing where you can do better, trying fresh approaches, and being kind to yourself in the process. For someone healing their inner child, personal growth strategies play an important role: they give you practical ways to address old fears, limited beliefs, or emotional habits that have held you back. Rather than feeling stuck in past patterns, you gain tools to move forward.

In this chapter, we will look at specific strategies for personal growth, explaining how they can help your emotional well-being and your relationship with your inner child. We will also talk about the mindsets and attitudes that allow these strategies to work best, as well as obstacles you might face along the way. By the end, you should have a fuller understanding of how to encourage your own growth and keep it going, even when life gets hard.

Why Personal Growth Strategies Are Important

1. **They Provide Direction**
   Without a plan or mindset aimed at improvement, you might feel adrift, responding to problems only as they appear. Growth strategies offer a more intentional approach, so you can choose goals and guide your decisions in a clear way.
2. **They Combat Old Wounds**
   Many people carry emotional pain from childhood—feelings of rejection, insecurity, or abandonment. Growth strategies help you actively work on these wounds, rather than letting them define your life.
3. **They Boost Self-Esteem**
   Each time you learn a new skill, manage an emotional trigger better, or expand your understanding of yourself, your sense of worth increases. This, in turn, reinforces your ability to keep growing.

4. **They Open You to New Possibilities**
   Growth often means stepping beyond what you thought you could do or who you believed you could be. Strategies aimed at personal development can reveal options you never considered.
5. **They Strengthen Inner Child Healing**
   By adopting healthier habits and thoughts, you show the younger side of you that positive change is possible. This can rewrite old beliefs about being stuck or helpless, offering hope and empowerment.

Mindsets That Support Personal Growth

1. **Willingness to Learn**
   You do not have to know everything at the start. A growth-focused mindset values learning from mistakes, feedback, or fresh experiences. It sees each stumble as a chance to gain insight, not a final verdict on your worth.
2. **Patience**
   Emotional changes do not happen overnight. Setting a calm, steady pace helps you avoid frustration when results take time. Each step forward matters.
3. **Honesty with Yourself**
   Real growth requires a clear view of what holds you back—old resentments, self-doubt, or unhelpful habits. Being honest does not mean blaming yourself harshly; it just means recognizing what is actually there so you can address it.
4. **Openness to Help**
   Personal growth does not mean doing it all alone. Sometimes, a friend, counselor, or mentor can offer insights you miss. Being open to help can speed your progress and prevent isolation.
5. **Flexibility**
   What works at one stage of healing might not work in the next. A flexible mindset allows you to adapt strategies as your needs evolve.

Strategy 1: Breaking Goals into Manageable Steps

1. **The Concept**
   People often create big goals like, "I want to overcome my social anxiety," or "I want to feel confident in who I am." These are great aims, but they can feel overwhelming. Breaking them into small, doable steps turns a big mountain into smaller hills you can climb one at a time.
2. **Why It Helps**
   - Reduces overwhelm by giving you clear, tiny tasks.
   - Creates more opportunities to experience small wins, which build momentum.
   - Lessens the chance of giving up because you see progress more frequently.
3. **How to Do It**
   - Define the big goal (e.g., "I will feel safer in social settings").
   - Brainstorm mini-steps (like greeting one coworker daily, then speaking in a small meeting, then trying a casual group event).
   - Decide a rough timeline for each step, but stay flexible if you need more practice at a certain stage.
   - Note each completion in a journal or a reminder app to track growth.
4. **Inner Child Link**
   Small steps are gentle. They respect that the child in you may feel anxious about large changes. Gradual progress reassures this younger side that you will not force big leaps too soon.

Strategy 2: Thought Restructuring

1. **The Concept**
   Thought restructuring involves identifying unhelpful or distorted thinking patterns and replacing them with more balanced thoughts. It does not mean forced optimism but rather seeing events more accurately, without the filter of past trauma or fear.
2. **Common Distorted Thoughts**
   - **All-or-Nothing Thinking**: "If I fail once, I'm useless."
   - **Mind Reading**: "They think I'm annoying," with no real proof.
   - **Overgeneralizing**: "This always happens—I never succeed."

- **Labeling**: "I'm just a loser."

3. **Why It Helps**
   Negative thought loops can lock you into old beliefs about not being good enough or being unlovable. Restructuring these thoughts can ease anxiety, shame, or anger, allowing you to respond to situations with a clearer head.
4. **How to Do It**
   - **Catch the Thought**: Notice a strong emotional spike and ask what thought is behind it.
   - **Question It**: Ask, "Is this always true?" "What proof do I have?" "Am I ignoring a different angle?"
   - **Replace It**: Form a more balanced thought. For example, instead of "I always fail," say, "Sometimes I struggle, but I've had successes, too."
   - **Practice**: Repeatedly counter the distorted thought whenever it appears, slowly training your mind to shift to more realistic thinking.
5. **Inner Child Link**
   Children often develop negative beliefs about themselves when they do not receive enough reassurance. Correcting these beliefs in adulthood helps heal that child's sense of self. Each time you replace a self-defeating thought with a balanced view, you reinforce a kinder message to your inner child.

Strategy 3: Emotional Regulation Techniques

1. **The Concept**
   Emotional regulation means managing strong feelings like anger, fear, or sadness in a healthy way. It does not imply ignoring or denying emotions, but rather feeling them and choosing safe ways to express them.
2. **Methods**
   - **Breathing Exercises**: Slow inhales and exhales to calm the nervous system.
   - **Grounding Exercises**: Focusing on the present, like describing objects around you, to reduce panic or flashbacks.
   - **Safe Outlets**: Writing, drawing, or physical outlets (like taking a brisk walk) to release tension.

   - **Pause and Reflect**: Waiting a few seconds or minutes before responding when you feel triggered.
3. **Why It Helps**
   Childhood hurts can leave you quick to anger, panic, or shame. Having emotional regulation methods close at hand helps you avoid impulsive reactions that make problems worse.
4. **How to Keep Them Handy**
   - Create a short list of your favorite techniques.
   - Practice them in calm times, so they become more natural when you are stressed.
   - Place reminders in your home or phone—like "Breathe" or "Take a step back."
5. **Inner Child Link**
   By learning to hold and soothe your feelings, you act like the supportive adult figure that might have been missing in your younger years. You show the child within that big emotions can be handled safely, not pushed away or punished.

Strategy 4: Regular Self-Review Sessions

1. **The Concept**
   A self-review session is when you spend time—maybe once a week or once a month—looking at how you are doing. You examine your mood, progress on goals, triggers that arose, and any lessons learned.
2. **What to Include**
   - **Successes**: Note areas where you felt stronger or handled a problem better.
   - **Difficult Moments**: Identify triggers or events that brought up old emotional wounds or confusion.
   - **Action Steps**: Outline ideas for how to handle these triggers next time.
   - **Adjustments**: Consider whether you need to tweak your goals, try new techniques, or seek help from a friend or professional.
3. **Why It Helps**
   Reflection prevents you from drifting. It keeps you aware of changes in your emotions and progress. It also helps you celebrate small wins and see patterns you might miss in daily life.

4. **How to Do It**
    - Schedule a brief time slot: 15–30 minutes, maybe on a weekend.
    - Use a journal or digital document. Write down key thoughts on the points above.
    - If you find repeating triggers or stuck points, plan to focus on them in the coming week or month.
    - Keep these records to track your long-term journey.
5. **Inner Child Link**
   Periodic check-ins are like a caring adult asking a child, "How have you been? Is anything bothering you? Did anything good happen?" This consistent attention can mend neglect the child might have experienced in the past.

Strategy 5: Trying New Experiences

1. **The Concept**
   Often, old wounds or beliefs keep us in a small comfort zone. Trying new experiences—whether it is a hobby, a group event, or a skill—can open your eyes to fresh possibilities and foster personal growth.
2. **Why It Helps**
    - Challenges negative beliefs like "I can't do anything new" or "People will mock me."
    - Builds self-confidence as you realize you are more capable than you thought.
    - Adds variety and fun, which can lighten emotional burdens.
3. **How to Choose**
    - Start small: maybe attend a free local workshop, test a simple online class, or join a casual sports meetup.
    - Pick something that sparks at least mild curiosity.
    - Bring a supportive friend if you feel very nervous.
4. **Coping with Anxiety**
    - Use emotional regulation methods beforehand.
    - Break the event into phases: traveling there, greeting one person, staying a short time, etc.
    - Reward yourself afterward for trying.
5. **Inner Child Link**
   The child within often loves to explore, learn, and play. New experiences

can reignite that sense of wonder, telling your younger self, "We are allowed to discover and enjoy."

Obstacles to Personal Growth and How to Handle Them

1. **Lack of Time**
    - **Issue**: You feel swamped by work, family, or daily tasks, leaving no space for personal growth.
    - **Solution**: Start with micro-habits—5 minutes a day is still better than none. You can expand if you see benefits.
2. **Perfectionism**
    - **Issue**: You think you must do everything flawlessly or not at all.
    - **Solution**: Embrace the motto "Good enough is good enough." Growth is not about perfection but about gradual improvement.
3. **Fear of Failure**
    - **Issue**: Old experiences or beliefs make you dread trying new methods in case you "fail."
    - **Solution**: Redefine failure as feedback. If something does not work, you learn what to tweak. Use self-compassion, not harsh blame.
4. **Isolation**
    - **Issue**: You try to grow alone but get stuck or discouraged.
    - **Solution**: Consider a support group, a counselor, or at least one friend who understands your goals. Sharing insights can motivate you to keep going.
5. **Deep-Rooted Trauma**
    - **Issue**: If you have experienced major abuse or neglect, basic strategies might not be enough to heal hidden wounds.
    - **Solution**: Seek professional help. Personal growth strategies still help, but severe trauma often requires specialized counseling or therapy.

Real-Life Stories of Personal Growth Strategies in Action

1. **Case: Neha's Shift in Self-Talk**
    - **Situation**: Neha always told herself she was not worth much if her work was not perfect.

    - **Strategy**: She used thought restructuring, catching each "I failed" moment and countering it with, "I made a mistake, but I can fix it."
    - **Result**: Over months, Neha's anxiety about perfection eased. She also noticed a drop in procrastination. Her inner child felt safer taking small risks.
2. **Case: Tyler's Weekly Self-Review**
    - **Situation**: Tyler felt lost and scattered, with no sense of direction.
    - **Strategy**: He began a Sunday evening self-review: rating his mood for the week, listing triggers, and planning small tasks for the next week.
    - **Result**: The process revealed a clear pattern of tension whenever he interacted with a critical family member. He realized he needed firmer boundaries. By making small boundary-setting goals, Tyler felt more in control.
3. **Case: Janelle's First Group Class**
    - **Situation**: Janelle feared meeting new people, feeling they would judge her.
    - **Strategy**: She chose to break this fear by trying a pottery class for beginners. She used emotional regulation (deep breaths) before stepping into the studio.
    - **Result**: Though she was nervous at first, she found the group supportive. She left feeling proud for attending. It fed her curiosity about other creative courses.

Practical Exercises for Personal Growth

Exercise 1: The 1% Improvement List

1. Choose an area you want to improve—maybe managing impatience or feeling calmer in the morning.
2. Ask: "What is one small action (just 1% improvement) I can take to be better at this?"
3. Write down three or four ideas. For instance, to manage impatience: "Pause for five seconds before responding when I'm annoyed," or "Take a mini-break when I feel my anger rising."
4. Try one idea at a time for at least a week, then reflect on how it went.

Exercise 2: Daily Positives

1. At the end of each day, jot down one thing you did that shows growth, no matter how small. Maybe you comforted yourself instead of scolding yourself, or you calmly set a boundary.
2. If you forget, place a reminder note somewhere visible.
3. Over time, noticing these positives helps you see progress that might otherwise be invisible.

Exercise 3: Mind Map of Possibilities

1. Take a large sheet of paper (or use a mind-mapping tool).
2. Write the main area you want to grow in at the center (e.g., "Confidence in Speaking").
3. Draw branches for different approaches: "Small talk with strangers," "Join a speaking club," "Record voice notes," "Practice in a mirror," etc.
4. For each branch, add smaller ideas or resources (YouTube tutorials, supportive friend, an online group).
5. Glance at your map occasionally to remind yourself there are many ways to grow.

Lesser-Known Tips for Continual Progress (Extra Useful Insights)

1. **Seasonal Checkpoints**
   - Every change of season, spend an hour reviewing your mental state, major life events, and personal growth steps. This bigger-picture view can reveal if you are on track or need new goals.
2. **Use Audio and Visual Cues**
   - Sometimes words alone do not motivate you. Try short music snippets or simple pictures that symbolize the growth you want. For instance, a photo of a seed growing into a plant can remind you that slow progress is natural.
3. **Engage Multiple Senses**
   - If certain scents (like lavender) calm you, combine them with your reflection time. If certain textures (like a soft blanket) help you feel

safe, use them when exploring painful feelings. Multi-sensory approaches often deepen emotional work.

4. **Create Micro-Challenges**
   - Challenge yourself to do one small brave act each day—like speaking up once in a meeting, or trying a new recipe if cooking is outside your comfort zone. These micro-challenges quickly stack up into bigger confidence boosts.
5. **Document the Journey**
   - Take occasional pictures, create scrapbooks, or keep digital files that reflect your progress. This can be especially helpful for creative or physical goals, but it can work for emotional growth, too—capturing quotes, mood charts, or reflection passages.

Handling Setbacks and Plateaus

1. **Recognize Setbacks as Normal**
   Healing is not a straight line. You might have days or weeks where old habits return. That does not erase your progress; it is a signal to revisit your strategies, rest, or seek extra help.
2. **Avoid All-or-Nothing Thinking**
   If you slip up once, do not label yourself a failure. Growth is about trying again. Remind yourself of the progress you have made so far.
3. **Check for Stress Overload**
   Sometimes a plateau or backward step happens because you are too tired or dealing with new life demands. Adjust your goals or routines temporarily, focusing on simpler tasks until you regain balance.
4. **Renew Motivation**
   Go back to your reasons for wanting personal growth—maybe you want healthier relationships, improved mood, or a sense of peace. Let those reasons refill your determination.
5. **Take Breaks When Needed**
   Overpushing can lead to burnout. If you feel emotionally exhausted, allow a short pause from intense inner work, then pick it up again when you feel ready.

How Personal Growth Supports the Inner Child Long-Term

Each time you adopt a new strategy, you model for your inner child that you are capable of change and that you value a better life. Instead of living by old, painful stories, you write new chapters—ones where you handle discomfort with resilience or ask for help instead of suffering alone. Over time, these personal growth strategies become part of your identity, showing the child within that people can learn, heal, and find hope despite early wounds. This consistent effort changes the default narrative from "I'm stuck in my past" to "I can shape my future."

Conclusion of Chapter 19

Personal growth strategies are like tools you keep in a toolbox. They help you break large goals into smaller tasks, question distorted thoughts, regulate emotions, review your progress, and try new experiences. Used alongside supportive mindsets—like patience and openness to learning—these strategies can transform how you approach life's ups and downs.

While every step forward is important, do not be discouraged by slow progress or occasional setbacks. Growth in emotional healing is often a winding road, but each skill you gain strengthens your inner child's sense of security. In the final chapter, we will learn about long-term maintenance: how to sustain these changes, avoid slipping back into old patterns, and stay on a nurturing path for years to come.

CHAPTER 20: LONG-TERM MAINTENANCE

Introduction

You have explored many chapters now—understanding childhood wounds, discovering emotional care, setting boundaries, developing self-kindness, and practicing personal growth strategies. The question remains: How do you keep these positive changes alive for the long run? Life events can challenge your new habits, and old triggers can reappear. Long-term maintenance is about preserving the good you have gained, staying mindful of your inner child's needs, and adapting as your life evolves.

In this final chapter, we will talk about how to keep your healing steady once you have built a foundation. We will look at ways to handle future stressors, monitor your progress, and address any slips that happen over time. We will also review the importance of continuously offering safety and kindness to your younger self. By the end, you should feel prepared to carry forward the insights and skills you have gained, knowing that healing is an ongoing, yet deeply rewarding, process.

Why Long-Term Maintenance Matters

1. **Prevents Relapse into Old Patterns**
   Without consistent reminders and actions, old ways of thinking or reacting can creep back. Long-term maintenance ensures you do not lose the ground you have covered.
2. **Adapts to Life Changes**
   Major events—like job transitions, relationship shifts, or new responsibilities—can require you to adjust your healing practices. Ongoing maintenance helps you stay flexible.
3. **Builds Deeper Self-Trust**
   Each month or year you remain committed to your well-being, your inner child sees that your care is not temporary. This can lead to a stronger, more stable sense of worth.

4. **Supports Higher Goals**
   As you feel more secure, you may aim for bigger dreams—new relationships, creative pursuits, or career growth. Maintaining your emotional foundation lets you face these challenges with confidence.
5. **Promotes Overall Health**
   Emotional well-being connects to physical health, relationship quality, and general life satisfaction. Sustaining your healing practices can improve many areas of your life over time.

Key Elements of Long-Term Maintenance

1. **Consistent Routines**
   - We covered routines previously. Sticking to them, even at a lighter level, keeps you anchored.
   - Examples: journaling a few times a week, doing a monthly reflection, or continuing a short relaxation exercise daily.
2. **Periodic Check-Ins**
   - Schedule a self-review—maybe monthly or quarterly—to see how you are feeling, whether your triggers are different, or if you have new goals.
   - These check-ins can also reveal if you are slipping into unhelpful habits, so you can catch them early.
3. **Continual Learning**
   - Keep your mind open to new information about mental health, self-care, or relationship skills. Read articles, watch talks, or take short courses.
   - Learning new approaches stops you from getting stuck and can refresh your motivation.
4. **Support Systems**
   - Whether it is a friend, family member, counselor, or a support group, keep people in your circle who respect your journey.
   - Share both triumphs and difficulties with them. Hearing an outside perspective can keep you grounded.
5. **Self-Coaching**
   - As explained in the previous chapter, regularly guiding yourself remains crucial. Prompt yourself to reflect, ask helpful questions, and encourage yourself when facing uncertainty.

Handling Future Stressors

1. **Build a Crisis Plan**
   - Identify what to do if you feel overwhelmed again—who to call, what coping tools to use, where to find a safe space.
   - Write it down, so you are not scrambling for ideas in the moment.
2. **Review Past Wins**
   - Recall times you handled stress better than expected. Note which methods worked and keep them ready for the next challenge.
   - This reminder can lower panic and help you realize you have managed tough situations before.
3. **Use Preventive Techniques**
   - If you know a busy season or stressful event is coming, plan extra self-care or check-ins. For instance, if you have a family gathering that could trigger old wounds, schedule an extra therapy session or plan a relaxing activity afterward.
4. **Practice Flexibility**
   - Stress can disrupt routines. Be ready to modify them rather than drop them completely. For example, if you cannot do a full journaling session, write a few lines in a phone note.
   - A shortened version is better than nothing and keeps the habit alive.
5. **Watch for Warning Signs**
   - Some signs might be trouble sleeping, feeling on edge, or withdrawing from friends. If you see these patterns return, take action early—revise your self-care plan or reach out for help.

Keeping the Inner Child Safe Over Time

1. **Ongoing Affirmations**
   - Simple statements like, "I care about you, and I listen to you," directed to your younger self, can be repeated whenever you sense old fears or sadness.
2. **Safe Spaces and Objects**
   - Maintain or refresh the physical reminders that comfort your inner child—like a cozy blanket, a small stuffed toy, or a piece of artwork.

    - If you move or your living situation changes, recreate a small corner or shelf that feels welcoming.
3. **Gentle Response to Triggers**
    - Even after much healing, certain triggers can still pop up. When they do, respond calmly: "I know this is scary, but I can handle it."
    - Over time, these repeated reassurances strengthen the child's trust in your adult self.
4. **Healthy Self-Expression**
    - Keep an outlet for your younger side, such as occasional drawing or writing letters to your past self. This helps you remain aware of and responsive to any lingering sadness or needs.
5. **New Experiences Together**
    - When you try something enjoyable—like visiting a nature spot or playing a simple game—invite your inner child along in your mind. Imagine them looking through your eyes, sharing the excitement. This bonds you and replaces negative memories with more positive ones.

Staying Motivated for the Long Haul

1. **Notice Gradual Gains**
    - Healing changes often appear little by little. You might find you handle criticism better, or your self-talk is less harsh. When you spot these shifts, pause to appreciate them.
2. **Set Fresh Goals**
    - Once you have made progress, you might create new aims to keep growing. Maybe you work on deeper relationships, start a creative project, or volunteer in a community activity.
3. **Reward Consistency**
    - Acknowledge yourself when you maintain your routines for a certain period or use a coping skill effectively. Rewards can be small treats, free time to do something fun, or simply giving yourself a mental pat on the back.
4. **Stay Open to Adjustments**
    - If you become bored or feel stalled, tweak your routines or try a new self-reflection method. Sticking to the exact same plan forever can cause you to lose engagement.

5. **Inspire Yourself with Others' Stories**
    - Books, interviews, or talks from people who have worked through similar wounds can remind you that healing is possible. Their journeys can offer fresh tools and keep your hope alive.

Handling Relapse or Slips

1. **Acknowledge It Calmly**
    - If you find yourself returning to an old habit—say, lashing out in anger or shutting down emotionally—try not to panic. Recognize it as a slip, not a permanent failure.
2. **Identify the Trigger**
    - Ask what sparked the relapse. Was it a stressful week, a health issue, or an argument with a loved one? Understanding the cause helps you address it more directly.
3. **Revisit Core Practices**
    - Return to your foundational methods—basic routines, journaling, emotional regulation, or boundary-setting. Often, slips happen when these habits weaken.
4. **Seek Extra Help if Needed**
    - If the slip is serious or you feel stuck, consider a therapy tune-up session or reach out to a support group. A short period of extra guidance can get you back on track.
5. **Practice Self-Forgiveness**
    - Dwelling on guilt or shame can trap you. Instead, remind yourself that everyone falls into old patterns sometimes. The main thing is you recognized it and are working to correct it.

Situations That Often Test Long-Term Maintenance

1. **Major Life Changes**
    - Moving, a new job, marriage, divorce, or becoming a parent—these big shifts can unsettle your routines and emotional balance. Re-commit to self-care during transitions.
2. **Loss or Grief**

    - The death of a loved one or a major disappointment can trigger old wounds. Give yourself time and space, and lean on the coping tools you have gathered.
3. **Physical Health Problems**
    - Chronic illness or sudden health issues can drain your mental energy. If needed, adjust your goals temporarily to focus on recovery. Keep simple emotional care routines even if your physical stamina is lower.
4. **Changes in Support Network**
    - Friends may move away, or you might lose contact with a mentor or counselor. This can leave you feeling adrift. Seek new sources of connection or professional advice if necessary.
5. **Unexpected Triggers**
    - Sometimes a random smell, sound, or event can bring up buried memories. Remind yourself that you have survived before. Use grounding techniques and, if needed, talk it through with a safe person.

Real-Life Examples of Long-Term Maintenance

1. **Case: Aaron's Yearly Personal Retreat**
    - **Approach**: Each year, Aaron sets aside one weekend to go on a simple retreat—perhaps staying in a quiet cabin or even a small hotel room in his own city. During this time, he reviews how the past year went, reads old journal entries, and updates his goals.
    - **Outcome**: This yearly habit keeps him focused on growth and helps him notice if he has fallen back into old insecurities. He returns feeling renewed and more aware of what he wants to do next.
2. **Case: Melissa's Support Circle**
    - **Approach**: After therapy, Melissa joined a local wellness group that meets once a month. The group shares resources, discusses challenges, and celebrates personal wins.
    - **Outcome**: Knowing she has a monthly check-in encourages Melissa to keep up her progress. When she faces a setback, she recalls she can discuss it at the next meeting, so she remains accountable and avoids isolating herself.

3. **Case: Don's Plan for Stressful Periods**
    - **Approach**: Don works in a field that has seasonal deadlines. During those busy months, he knows his stress spikes and his self-care often slips. He created a "stress plan," which lists two quick relaxation methods, one friend to call for support, and a 5-minute nightly journaling routine.
    - **Outcome**: While these busy times still feel stressful, Don no longer crashes emotionally afterward. He has fewer anxiety episodes, and he manages to keep a baseline level of calm. This stability supports his inner child, reminding him that adult Don is in control even under pressure.

Practical Exercises for Long-Term Maintenance

Exercise 1: Seasonal Review

1. At the start of each new season (or every three months), set aside 30 minutes.
2. Reflect on your emotional state, major events of the past season, and any goals you completed or left unfinished.
3. Write a short plan for the next season: Are there new routines to try, habits to refresh, or areas where you need outside help?
4. Keep these seasonal notes in a folder to track your long-term growth story.

Exercise 2: Emotional Safety Checklist

1. List at least five things that help you feel secure—like certain music, a cozy blanket, a few supportive friends, or a breathing exercise.
2. Next to each item, note when you might use it (e.g., "When anxious before bedtime, I listen to calming music").
3. Post this checklist somewhere accessible. Each time you feel unsettled, check one or two items and follow through.

Exercise 3: Goal Renewal

1. Every few months, revisit your major goals. Ask, "Does this goal still serve me?" and "Have I learned something new that changes my direction?"
2. If you are satisfied with your progress, set a slightly higher or deeper goal. If you have lost interest in a goal, see if you can modify it or replace it with a more relevant aim.
3. This prevents stagnation and ensures your efforts match your current phase of life.

Lesser-Known Approaches to Sustain Healing

1. **Gratitude Letters**
   - From time to time, write a note to a person (past or present) who has supported you. You do not have to send it, but the act of writing fosters positive feelings and reminds you of the connections that matter.
2. **Mental "Time Capsules"**
   - If you face a big decision or transition, write a letter to your future self explaining your hopes and mindset right now. Set a date (months or years away) to read it. This can reveal how much you have grown.
3. **Creative Visualization**
   - Occasionally visualize an older, wiser version of yourself looking back on these times. Imagine what advice that future self might offer. This perspective can encourage patient long-term thinking.
4. **Theme Months**
   - Assign a personal growth theme to each month or quarter. For example, "Confidence in Communication," "Gentle Self-Talk," or "Healthy Routines." Focus your reading, practices, and reflections on that theme.
5. **Shared Projects**
   - Work on a short creative project or volunteer effort with people who also care about emotional growth. Collaborating can keep you accountable and add variety to your healing path.

Conclusion of Chapter 20

Long-term maintenance is not about being perfect or never feeling pain again. Rather, it is about preserving the progress you have made, preparing for life's stresses, and continuing to care for the child within you. Over time, the habits, routines, and mindsets you have built become second nature. This does not mean you will not face setbacks, but you will face them with stronger tools, deeper understanding, and more compassion.

As you step beyond these chapters and into daily life, remember that healing is an ongoing process. You have gained an array of methods to reduce shame, guilt, and fear; to set boundaries; to coach yourself with kindness; to engage in play and creativity; and to pursue personal growth. All these build a stable base for you to keep growing, day by day. Keep refining your strategies, remain open to outside help, and never forget to address your inner child's well-being. In doing so, you honor both who you were and who you are becoming—living proof that change is possible and worthy of sustained care.

www.ingramcontent.com/pod-product-compliance
Lightning Source LLC
LaVergne TN
LVHW012104070526
838202LV00056B/5619
* 9 7 8 3 7 5 9 8 9 0 8 7 0 *